Adventures with My Mouse

Seniors and Pre-seniors Make It Happen with Internet Dating

Marti DiGioia
with Rob Ruggles

ISBN: 1461089689
ISBN-13: 9781461089681
Library of Congress Control Number 2011905995
CreateSpace, North Charleston, South Carolina

The names and places have been changed to respect
the privacy of those involved.

Table of Contents

Acknowledgements

My friends kept questioning me about my Internet dating. They were so curious, yet hesitant to try it. They wanted to know more. I thank them for their persistent curiosity that inspired this book.

The CreateSpace Project Team from Amazon knew how to guide this novice writer. I appreciate their professionalism and their availability to answer my many questions.

Close friends did the early editing: Jan Summers, Kathy Bowser, and Tom Cates. Their suggestions and encouragement were vital to my continued creativity.

To the men I met, particularly those who took part in the survey to share their experiences, thank you all.

I am grateful to my loving family who kept my enthusiasm flowing.

Introduction

It was a prolonged journey toward my goal of finding someone special for this period in my life. I was traveling on my own but surrounded by participants and observers. At the start, it seemed easy for others who said, "We met on the Internet," but that road is not easy. It involves time and energy, as does any worthwhile life-changing endeavor.

The Internet dating game has no geographical boundaries and very few ethical ones.

You're out there on your own, making life-decision choices with a keyboard, a comfy chair, your eyeglasses, and a cup of coffee on the side.

With no book of instructions, you must select the most effective sites. Daunting choices are available. Do I post a picture? Should I write a cute profile or a deadly serious one? How do I know if and when it's safe to meet someone in person? What if I fall in love with a Mr. Right who lives on the other side of the country?

My friends were afraid to try the Internet world, but they wanted to know every detail of my own experiences, living it vicariously where wise women feared to tread.

There are many helpful guides for younger daters but few for those of us who have retired and are ready to spend time creating a new and final relationship, or the single parent who has raised the children and is now ready for some selfish pleasures. Do we want a casual or a serious relationship? Are we just lonely enough to give it a try within the safe boundaries of an anonymous mode? Are we looking for a friendly, attentive pen pal?

It became evident after several years of dating that a guide book would help all those "almost, not quite" adventurers. Although I was older than some when I started this journey, the book is geared for use by any person who appreciates the benefits of a close relationship.

My most positive result of this exploration was binding with a very special person who has become very dear to me, my Good Knight, Rob Ruggles. He will join us in this guide. We hope it will inform you as you adventure to your desired destination.

Make It Happen!

Marti DiGioia

Chapter 1—Conception

Planting the Seed

What was the trigger? Why would an independent seventy-one-year-old woman who was quite satisfied with her status quo suddenly decide to enter the Internet dating scene? After two productive marriages, I was well into a gratifying career and enjoying all types of selfish pursuits. I could watch television with total control of the remote. I had been single for two-thirds of my life and had developed a lifestyle tailor made for me. Now retired, I was half-heartedly reflecting on the possibility of sharing my unaccustomed spare time with a yet-to-be-found special person. But where to start?

It came about quite innocently. I was daydreaming while taking my evening walk. My mind filled with a prophetic vision: there I was, in my rocking chair on the porch of the nursing home, all ninety-five years of me. I reflected on the past, and a widowhood or twenty-two years dominated my thoughts. Why hadn't I checked into dating? Why had I put a career ahead of the comfort of a committed relationship? Now it was too late.

Although I shook myself out of the daydream, the provocative questions remained.

During my career days, I put a framed banner on the wall of my office. It showed a baseball player sliding into base, and the caption read, "Make It Happen!" That had been my motto for years, and it was time to take it out of the office and into my personal life. At the age of seventy-one, I knew that I should take action immediately.

A day later, serendipity stepped in. As I watched a morning news program I saw a nice-looking retired couple being interviewed. They met on the Internet. There it was: my answer! No need to settle for the local menu or the questionable bar scene.

Game Plan

The interview of the happy couple was barely finished when I bolted to my computer to get started. I searched for "dating" and was astounded at all the choices. I needed to find something geared for seniors. Fortunately, the site names contain clues, and I found that I could choose by region, religion, or age.

I decided on Senior People Meet. All I had to do was hit "Search," and a smorgasbord of potentials appeared, but wait, it wasn't that easy. First I had to fill in the provided form for user name and password. I sat staring at the screen, stared a while longer, and realized that I was having a problem with going public. Heaven help me if the local neighborhood found out that this well-respected old lady was "going online" to publicly offer herself for who knows what. My upbringing required that a woman respond to a male overture. We were never allowed to call the boys, and if no one invited you to the prom, you didn't go. An "old maid" accepted her status without any thought of becoming the pursuer. Was I ready to forsake that early training and enter this new world of dating? My mind went back to the happy couple that were part of my original inspiration. They were raised in my era and certainly seemed pleased to have updated their beliefs. I took a deep breath and recommitted to Make It Happen.

For a user name, I chose "On the Avenue," which sounded original and had a sophisticated ring. A message popped up: "Sorry, that password is taken." The suggestion was given to choose "On the Avenue" followed by several numbers. I decided to add 333, which was a much earlier street address of mine dating back to those innocent days of "wait for the boys to call." I was ready to enter a new era in my personal history.

I was ready to see the contestants anxiously awaiting my arrival. No, not yet: I had to fill out another form, which asked for my Headline, something catchy to attract that right person. Again, I spent a long time staring at the screen. I finally decided to hit it dead on with "Ready, Set, Go!" If I was going to Make It Happen, I had to jump right in there. Up came a long, tedious listing of information about my preferences in looks, interests, activities, marital status, income, and so on. Was I looking for casual dating or a long-term relationship? The site included some help to guide me through the maze of checking my preferred attributes.

I had to tell about myself and what I wanted in a mate. Talk about a challenge. I came from the school of being modest about oneself: "Don't toot your own horn." Could my marketing career self take over? Make It Happen. I started writing.

"Want the best? Tired of cranky, overpowering women?" I don't think so. There had to be a happy medium. Honest, direct, with the hope of commanding attention—that's what I would find attractive in a male counterpart. It wasn't easy. The words had to strongly attract and become the foreplay for later action. After many false starts, including the melodramatic "Life's highway is a lonely road when walked alone," I finally settled on the following:

"I'm a lady in waiting for that just right man. In return he will find me to be caring, enthusiastic, inquiring, energetic, witty, a problem solver, teacher, fun-loving with best friend potential. Ideally the just right man will instinctively know when to give me independent moments and when to be close for comfort and sharing. We will be tolerant of each other's less-than-perfect attributes. A solid, approving friendship will begin our successful relationship."

Way to go. I liked it, but would he? Gotta try. After all, this was just the opening commercial. The drama would unfold in later emails when specific questions would be answered. I hit the button to submit all this and waited for it to be approved, within twenty-four hours. Could I sit back and relax? No way.

I was invited to search . . . wait a minute, give the age, geographical area, and any other pertinent requirements so that the site could find my Mr. Right. I selected sixty-eight to seventy-six years within fifty miles of home.

Finally, I was on my way. The available gentlemen appeared on my screen, ripe for the picking. Some had pictures, others just the outline of a perfectly shaped male upper torso. (I was amused that none of these torsos had the more typical imperfectly shaped potbelly.) Their headlines were included along with the instruction to "Click here" if I was impelled to see the rest of the profile. I could see the times when they were last online (Online Now, Within 24 Hours, 2 Weeks, 3 Months).

Action

Here we go. This one looked inviting. Close to home. Seventy-four, five foot eight, average body type, Christian, Caucasian. Doesn't smoke, drinks socially, retired, Masters degree. Looking good. "I love to play tennis year round." Darn. I needed a golfer.

I tried another one. Seventy, six foot two, could lose a few pounds, smoker. Red flag! I gave up smoking and couldn't be around it.

The next headline read, "Let's play a round of golf." Bingo! This might be it. Seventy-one, good looking, social drinker, non-smoking. Christian, Caucasian, looking for a long-term relationship, legally separated. Legally separated? I didn't think that was possible in Pennsylvania. Forget Mr. Polygamous. I told myself to not get discouraged and that "someday my prince would come." I'd only just begun." Move on. Make It Happen.

Hallelujah! Here he was. Look at that picture. Blue eyes that could melt ice cream in the Arctic. A fringe of white hair. Bald had never looked so good. He was seventy years old, healthy and active, exercising four times a week. His list of activities and interests were a mirror image of mine. His preferred age for women was fifty to sixty-five, but I was as active as any one of those. Truly we were meant for each other. He hadn't been on the site for three months, which meant that he would be happy to hear from me.

I had the choice of sending a "flirt" and saw a list of opening lines—"I like your profile." "How about a cuppa Java?" "Ready for a soul mate?"—and others of that sort. I could write an original email to this marvelous candidate and thought this was the better choice. I was ready to jump right in there and Make It Happen.

"Hi LesteroftheLake,

Certainly was pleasurable to read your profile. Please check mine, and you will see what a perfect match we are. Do you live right on the lake and do you go fishing? I used to fish regularly, but now I don't have a fishing buddy." (No, scratch that last sentence . . . it sounded needy.) I really enjoyed fishing the Canadian lakes, mainly in Ontario . . . great bass and pike. Nothing better than a fresh fish dinner, swimming in the afternoon, and frying in the pan that night." (That was better, a little more upbeat.) I'm quite new to this style of dating, just a babe in the woods! (How was that for virginal?) Sure would like to hear from you. Until then, On the Avenue333."

On this fateful day, I kept checking my computer with great anticipation. Any return message? No. Again, no. Once again, no. Maybe he'd gone fishing. Maybe that evening I would hear. The hours hang heavy when you're waiting for Mr. Just Right to reply. I checked once more before bed. Nothing.

Set Back

As the long days passed, anticipation faltered, fears of rejection rose. I hesitated to contact anyone else because LesteroftheLake seemed to be the perfect one. There was no sense getting some other guy all excited. I found myself reflecting on the damage done by rejection. I am an overachiever, not pleased with any result other than "above and beyond." Maybe Internet dating wasn't the way to go. I never figured on rejection! It appealed to me because the preselected men were also ready and waiting. Why else would they be on there? What if I was rejected by the next dozen men I contacted? Could I handle that? I thought back on my career in sales and marketing. I was now the product. I had to be willing to deal with being rejected by those who are not looking for my particular attributes. I realized that I wouldn't hesitate to reject a fellow that didn't meet my expectations. It is not as if I were breaking up with someone after a long relationship. I had to learn to accept rejection as a necessary part of this journey and not take it personally. During this heavy discussion with myself, I became curious about my competition.

I went back to Senior People Meet and checked in as a man looking for a woman for a long-term relationship, age fifty-five to seventy-five. What an interesting trip that was. I saw every shape, good looking and bad. The profiles hit heavily on "love to cook," "spoil my man," and "touchy feely." I came away feeling better about myself, my head held high, because my profile didn't fit the 1950s style of "little subservient woman." The diversity of choices was impressive; I was convinced that I fit in as one of the many *good* choices.

"Go for it", my overachieving self said! It was all a matter of screening and matching. What was a little rejection if it helped you achieve your goal? With renewed commitment and determination, I returned to the site to review all those waiting men.

A Rude Awakening

I scrolled down to see if there were any pictures that really appealed to me. There was one with really kind eyes. "Educated, retired, above average income, seventy-one, love my family. [So far, so good.] Drink socially, nonsmoker. Take care of my two grandchildren while their parents are at work. [What a sweet man.] Looking for that very special woman who will be a friend before a lover. Will treat her as a lady, putting her needs first." I could see that he was online and could click to chat directly. Why not?

I clicked, and a smaller screen popped up. I wrote, "Good morning. Nice profile. Would love to hear from you." I waited to see if he would respond. A few minutes went by . . . he was probably checking my profile. Finally, he responded,

"Hi, lovely lady, aren't you the cat's meow? Great profile. How far are you from the turnpike?"

"Not far at all, about five miles."

"Let's not waste time with words. I'd like to come see you. Once you feel the size of my cock you will be screaming for more!"

I reread it but still couldn't believe my eyes. I hit the "End" button as if it, too, were despicably defiling. I'm not a prude, but his gentlemanly profile had given me no advance warning of this type of response! I guess Internet dating means different opportunities to different people. After this "screen rape," I walked away from my computer.

There had to be some clue as to how to avoid "screen rape." I went back to the perpetrator's profile. In the user name, hotforu, the language of intent was exposed. Lesson learned: "Leave no word unturned." A part of me said, "Good for you, buddy, at least you were honest about it before I made any more contact." With some searching, I found more: oleman469, clitlover, fck4u. They were all lined up and ready for someone like "hottotrotlady."

I felt overwhelmed at the magnitude of this undertaking. There was more to it than pushing the buttons. It was time to broaden my knowledge and check some other sites. I could see that numbers would count: the more contacts made, the better the chance of one of them being Mr. Just Right.

Lessons Learned

I could have settled for the normal route of meeting that right person at the library, the produce counter, in photography class, or at church, but I wasn't content to sit and wait like so many other people do. I wanted to update my dating method to the newest and best mode. The Internet was my answer, and it could easily be yours. You must allow yourself to be the pursuer. There's no shame if you're the one who decides to Make It Happen.

This adventure is more involved than just placing an order and having it filled. The site has to be carefully researched before you use it, so let site selection work for you. If religion is of utmost importance, go to the site that focuses on religious preference. You will find an endless assortment of sites to match your desires. There are sites for millionaires, plus sizes, boy toys, medical professionals, country singles, vegetarians, prison inmates, single parents, herpes sufferers, scientists, asexual men and women, tall gay men, astrological matches, and hundreds more. Simply search Google for your choice. The established, general-interest sites are Match.com, eHarmony, Plenty of Fish, Yahoo Personals, and Senior People Meet. There are many more. Just search Google for senior dating or dating for Christians or pet lovers or whatever type you prefer.

You may want to look for someone in your area. It is much easier to start a relationship if you share some knowledge of places and find that you have friends in common. A four-hour drive or flight is not conducive to Saturday-night dates.

A creative, eye-catching user name and headline are vital. Be cautious that your user name does not imply false allure. Writing a profile that captures the heart of Prince Charming takes some time, thought, and effort. The ideal sequence of events is to write your profile and headline and select your user name before you visit a site intending to make selections. This will give you the time to really ponder and be creative instead of plowing into the scene unprepared.

Be highly critical of your profile. When you have finished it, be sure to double-check for spelling mistakes or incorrect verbs. Apply all you learned in your eighth-grade English class, and make any needed corrections.

As for LesteroftheLake, I realized later that a three-month hiatus from being online means that the person is gone forever.

A list of "must haves" and "must not haves" kept beside the computer screen will certainly help to weed out the nonqualifiers. It will save you from being lured into the wrong contact due to good looks or income level. "Must haves" are the most important characteristics you are looking for in a companion. List those qualities, starting with honesty, sincerity, or kindness, or whatever is a "must have" for you. Keep digging until you get to "tolerance for others" or "humor in difficult situations"—the nitty gritty that would make or break a relationship for you. Do the same with your "must not haves." Know your acceptable levels of negative characteristics. These are real people that you will be dealing with, not some idealistic fantasy that you create at your keyboard. Read their profiles critically. Before any contact is made, you will have screened each one to the best of your ability because you have predetermined your criteria. Obvious hints of a mismatch may be there, hidden behind those good looks. If he can't stand pets in the house, chances are that he will not make an exception for your irresistible kitten. If football games are a "must watch" for him but not for you, move on. Beginning a relationship with the hope of changing someone is like skating on cracked ice. Stay on track with your needs.

Be ready for heartbreak. If it happens, it's a bump in the road, not a black hole of never return.

I know now that this journey is more involved than clicking on someone's profile and riding off into the sunset. LesteroftheLake, where are you?

Chapter 2—Rob Tells His Side of the Story

There are two sides to every story. Here to give you the male side of this journey is my partner, Rob. In chapter 6, you will learn all about Rob and how we met, but for now we need a little background on what he was going through at the start of his Internet dating journey. It may answer the question of whether the scene is the same for men and women.

Hi, I'm Rob.

I wasn't the least bit interested in Internet dating. Unlike my coauthor, I wasn't looking to the future. My head and heart were in the past.

It had been four months since my beloved wife of forty-three years had passed away. JoAnn bravely fought cancer for eight long years. I sold my businesses and spent those last eight years making our lives together as gratifying as possible under the circumstances. In my mid-sixties, I was busy cleaning up estate matters, consolidating, and scaling back my life.

In retrospect, I was in the classic widower denial mode. In my mind, no one could ever replace JoAnn, her calm poised view of life, her kindness to all, her wonderful understated humor, and much, much more. I hadn't yet even considered the possibility of another relationship. The last thing on my agenda was a new commitment.

We had a lot of friends from our marriage and business. I had started getting invitations to dinners, parties, and so on to meet unattached "friends of friends." As flattering and good as all that was, the time just wasn't right. If I thought about it, why be involved with Internet dating when I had all these potential contacts? I had heard of Internet dating but knew very little about it. I probably thought something like, "That's for the losers and desperate souls."

One day, I was having lunch with Sam, an old friend of ours. I have to give you a little background on Sam before I tell you why this lunch became so significant. Bear with me.

He and his first wife had been our friends for over twenty years. When they divorced, we stayed in touch with both of them. While my wife was with us, we had dinner three or four times a year with Sam and his "lady of the moment." Sam's lady was always exceptional. Sam is, by most standards, rather exceptional himself. Good looking. Works out. A high-profile businessman known all around town. Dynamic and full of energy in his midfifties. At the peak of his career. It is easy to see how he would attract ladies. And what ladies! Not the "trophy wife" kind, but ladies who had interesting careers and accomplished lives of their own. Several physicians. A concert violinist/soloist and several artists. Several on-the-way-up executives. They were all quite handsome in their individual ways. After meeting each, on our drive home, JoAnn and I would compare notes. We were always in amazement, thinking, "This one's for Sam." Several of his ladies became friends of ours. Sam was never satisfied. He wasn't a lecher, he just didn't want to make a commitment.

Back to the lunch. We had been reliving memories of JoAnn. Sam asked me, "How are you doing? Ready to meet someone new? I have some good contacts." I confessed that my wife and I were amazed at the interesting ladies Sam knew. They were so diverse and interesting.

"How can you know so many interesting women, Sam?"

He replied, "I meet them on the Internet!"

That certainly gave me an entirely different view of Internet dating, both the type of people and the level of quality possible. It wasn't just for the losers and desperate souls.

While I was still in personal denial mode and not interested in a new relationship, I couldn't get Sam's revelation out of my head. It stayed in my mind, ready to be tapped when the moment was right. A month or so later, I looked up Internet dating on my computer. Wow!

The more I searched the Internet, the more options became available, from real top quality to gross. Sam later gave me some tips on finding positive relation-ships. The most memorable was this: "Play it straight. Be honest and sincere. You will not always be treated the same in return. That's the way you will filter out the wrong ones and find the right person." Several months later, I joined one of the major dating services, eHar-mony. I committed to a one year membership, filled out all the profiles, and got my analysis of what the recommended good matches for me would entail. Frankly, based on my advertising background and professional market research experiences, I was skeptical of some of the profiling.

I was taking a long-term approach. I felt that I should register and try this, but I wasn't actively seeking a relationship. Obviously, some curious denial syndrome was still at work, especially since I did not include my picture. (All Internet dating services note that adding a picture increases the response many fold.)

I sat back and waited to see who and what would respond, and I received a lot from all types. Probably, in retrospect, I was naïve to put in my profile that I was a recent widower and several other hot-button clues as to travel and affluence. I was so full of myself that I got quantity and not quality in responses. Many checked me out regardless of age or interests.

I wanted to fine-tune my profile, so I started by seeing what the other guys in my age bracket had in their profiles. What were they saying to attract the ladies? Shocker. Over fifty percent contained up-front sexual innuendo from the not-too-subtle to gross. Even still, there were, in my opinion, ones that projected honesty, sincerity, and openness that, as an ad man, I thought were convincing and had promise.

I went back, toned down my profile, and narrowed my preferences as to age, geography, interests, etc. While the temptation was great, I decided to play it straight in both my profile and responses. I would respond to every inquiry. I would be forthcoming and polite. I would send a "No, but thank you, and I wish you well" when I wasn't interested for whatever reason. I felt that, knowing they had at least warranted a response, they would feel better about themselves. I know I did.

One day a woman responded who lived within five miles of me, and she was a professional playwright. While I was never in the theater business except to advertise and promote plays, I've always loved live theater, so this contact was especially interesting and rather unexpected. We emailed back and forth for several weeks, and then I took The Big Step and suggested that we meet. Rather than meet over coffee (as I suggested), she chose a local theater where they were in rehearsal of one of her plays.

Anyone can claim that they're a playwright, but few can prove it with an actual performance. I was hooked. We met at the theater and watched the rehearsal, followed with supper. I was no longer looking back. I was looking forward thanks to the unexpected discovery of Internet dating.

The playwright and I had a great year together. She had a play produced off Broadway in New York that year, so we made lots of trips together to The Big Apple. We were in town during the September 11 attacks, which added an unforgettable dimension to the relationship.

My children were overjoyed that I had someone in my life, and life was becoming very good again. We parted friends after a year or so, but I knew exactly where to go and what to do for my next relationship.

Lessons Learned

What did I learn from my first foray into Internet dating? A lot, including the following:

Play it straight. If you truly want an honest relationship with a good person, you have to start with yourself. (Thank you, Sam.) You get what you give. Why waste your time or your respondents' time?

Give honest background information. Like age, interests, and so on. Again, why waste everybody's time? If you meet people, which is the goal, they will find out the truth for themselves. Give false information, and you will be back-pedaling the minute you meet. Why? Because you weren't honest with yourself or with them.

Be realistic about your preferences. Some older guys make it known that they're interested in very young women. They may be, but if one responds, do you think she has a good long-term relationship in mind? (Some guys never learn.) Consider geography. If you are not willing to travel across the state or to another region, why not put it in your preferences? Again, why waste time?

Play down the sex. This seems extremely difficult for many of my male peers. The anonymity of Internet dating seems to unleash unwarranted up-front sexual approaches. Some guys will hide behind that anonymity and say things they would never say face to face. Some Internet daters seem to forget they are seeking real people and real relationships. These up-front sexual statements are sexism at its worst and turn off women of any age. Again, why waste your time? There is a time for sexual expression, but it's not at the beginning of your Internet dating contact.

Internet dating is the breakthrough of our generation's love life. It expands the "universe" of possibilities our civilization never before imagined. We "oldies" have been given the opportunity never before possible: to select and meet an ever-expanding group of singles, of our own age and with our preferences, from the comfort of our homes. There are thousands of choices, where in decades past, we were lucky if we could even meet a handful. There truly is someone for everyone and truly a way to meet, share, and love that person today!

To some (too many) men: "C'mon guys, wise up." Especially the "mature" guys. In your later years, you are dealing with very experienced women. Often, they are far more experienced than you, because of multiple divorces and expiring husbands. The "lines" and sexual verbiage that might have worked when you were young with raging hormones will simply not work now, especially with today's women in our age bracket. (I doubt they really ever did work or evolve into good and/or long-term relationships.) Stop wasting everyone's time. Stop being gross. Stop making fools of yourselves.

The sexual part of any good relationship comes with time and demonstration of other qualities. Let's call it good mature sex. It is the best ever. Believe me.

Chapter 3—Maiden Voyage

Thank you, Rob. Isn't it interesting to see that we have many concerns in common as we travel this Internet dating road, and isn't it nice to run into a gentleman?!

Remembering

Time now to experience some of the results of my Internet dating. Time to meet some of the other real men who crossed my path as I was determined to Make It Happen. There were many "One Page Stands," the fellows that appeared with a flirt or a message and were immediately shot down by negatives in their profiles or who never returned after I responded. They were strangers passing in the night, never to know whether they might have clicked. You learn to accept this. You justify that if it were meant to be, it would have been, and you keep moving on.

I'd like to introduce you to several outstanding contacts that made a difference in that they helped propel me through the labyrinth of confusion in my return to the dating world. Get ready for a quick look at a selected few.

The Scene: Pittsburgh International Airport, 2:00 p.m. on a Tuesday in October.

Actors: A nervous me, Fred from South Carolina, and hundreds of resolute travelers.

Action: He came up the escalator from the baggage area carrying his overnight bag and sleep apnea case. He wasn't as tall as I had imagined, perhaps due to the forward thrust of his walk, as if heading into a wind storm. I quickly turned away, not quite ready for this real life meeting.

Fred and I first corresponded with lengthy emails, and then we spent many hours on the phone. He wasn't exactly what I was looking for, but he was definitely friendly and intelligent, and I was seduced by his anxiousness to meet me.

As he looped back again, looking for me, I took a deep breath and stepped forward, officially beginning my quest in real life. We exchanged exploratory smiles. There was no particular magic for me. We performed the expected hugs and "How are you's".

I offered, "Would you like to have coffee before we head out?"

"Sure, if you'll be my guest," he said, confirming my impression of "a gentleman."

We sat down in a crowded little coffee shop, and as we sipped away, I couldn't help but notice all the wrinkles around his face and neck. Was this all from southern sun? Or was this the face of the men I would now be seeing? They were not like the youths I dated so long ago. I wasn't sure that I was ready to accept this reality.

We continued to chat about our plans for his visit: wine and snacks on the porch, dinner, a spooky Halloween walk, a movie, more meals out (I avoid cooking meals—it might set a precedent!), and pecan pie and coffee with the family.

We headed for his motel, filling the silence with comments about the passing scenes. (I should claim a bonus from the Days Inn that housed Fred and subsequent guests over the next couple of years.) We dropped his belongings there and began our two-day "Get Acquainted and See If There's a Future" visit.

It was a surreal time. Remember those twenty-two years that I had gone without constant male companionship? This stranger who wrote the words and then spoke the words was now a living, breathing male body. We filled the time with a lot of walking around town and less talking than we had done on the phone. Our chemistry experiment was failing. We were like two unmatched test tubes trying our best to Make it Happen.

Panic hit when he said, "I think I could be happy in a little town like this." It was a little too close for comfort, and this fellow was too country for me.

I was relieved when Thursday finally came, and we left for the airport. A hurried peck on the cheek, and I was done.

His next email thanked me for the time that we spent together. He felt that before we took the relationship any further, he should admit that he was a smoker. I thought that I could smell a hint of cigarettes on his clothes, but he never smoked in my presence. He had listed "nonsmoker" in his profile. This was my out. I had stopped smoking some time ago and had no interest in being near a smoker. I immediately shared that with him. There was no need to further our relationship. It was a nice way to end without attacking personally. Sometimes you know beyond a doubt that a relationship is not right, and you prefer to exit without hurting the other person.

I knew I had to be more discerning about selection. I decided on an educated man, still working or not, Caucasian, ideally a fisherman and golfer, high energy, interested in the arts, travel, and a long-term relationship. I did not want a smoker or someone who had never married, was legally separated, a motorcyclist, or an atheist or agnostic. The list would grow as I became more experienced.

Renunciation

Enter Charlie to break my heart. Charlie was from New York State. He was a chemist, loved to fish and golf, had been divorced for four years, and was ready for a long-term relationship. We did the required writing and talking over a period of six weeks. All was well. He came to visit the second weekend in December, which is a magical time of year for me. Who could ask for a more-perfect setting?

We enjoyed several local Christmas music programs, one at the school, the other at one of the churches. I was proud to introduce him to friends who doubted the Internet dating scene. Now they could appreciate how clever I was to do this! Charlie was well received.

On Christmas Eve, we met my family for brunch at Denny's and had quite a congenial time. We spent each weekend together through mid-January.

After a rather loveless marriage, Charlie felt ill at ease in expressing his feelings, and he asked for help and nurturing because he wanted so badly to experience a truly loving relationship. A kiss in passing or a pat on the butt did not come naturally to him, but he wanted it to be that way. He wanted the encouragement of my coaching and touching to get him there. He was so open and lovable that I found the teaching role to be quite enjoyable.

I tend to express inner feelings by placing my hands on the computer keyboard and letting them move, as I had done for years on the piano keyboard. I sympathized with Charlie's struggle and expressed it thus:

On the Path
She stands at the corner, not sure of her way.
Is he standing beside her, has he fallen behind,
this hero, this lover, this one of a kind?

The past loveless years are slowing his pace,
Dare he move forward to an unknown place?
Will years slowly waste the intensity away?
She turns and senses his hesitant step.
Loving eyes meet his to quiet his mind,
this hero, this lover, this one of a kind.

Can present actions erase past years?
Can laughter dry regretful tears?
Can faltering steps grow steady in trust?
Taking the risk is a mighty big must.
She is patient, understanding, but now sure of herself,
As she slows her pace, dropping behind
this hero, this lover, this one of a kind.

No, I never showed this to him, but we seemed to share everything else. We talked about where we would live when we married. Charlie liked the idea of country living but close enough to the city for cultural events. "Think you would enjoy raising chickens?" he asked. "Okay," I replied, "as long as I don't have to wring their necks and eat them." I was delighted to watch him grow more at ease with our closeness. Laughter was easy and quiet was comfortable.

On a bleak, snowy January morning, I went to the computer to read his morning message. We had talked the night before and he had sounded tired; work had been demanding that week.

"Morning Marti, Sorry that I must put an end to our very fine relationship. By chance I ran into a very special lady a couple weeks ago. We had a close relationship a few years back. We have decided to see each other exclusively. To explain any further would be too heart-breaking for both you and me. Best to you, Charlie."

Good Lord, what was all that? I wrote back, asking for a detailed explanation but heard nothing. Cruel, unfair. I had had some doubts while we were together, hoping that Charlie could resolve his past problems before we made a final commitment, but I was sure he was The One and that I would never love again! My memories were only the totally happy ones—the laughter shared and the warmth of his touch. My best supposition is that he went back to his wife. Even after the divorce, they spent holidays and birthdays with the children, and there was still a strong tie between them.

Welcome to the ugly side of putting yourself out there! It was several weeks of tears and encouragement from family before I could return to my Make It Happen goal. I went back to the drawing board with reluctance but determined to recover.

Rebuilding

I had been writing to Wes before I found Charlie. We had been sending half-hearted emails back and forth at irregular intervals. I liked his straightforward profile, and his emails were always quite informative and humorous. I sent him a lengthy email about all my fun activities over Christmas, with not a word about a broken heart.

He wrote back, "I wondered where you went. Your emails were as slow in coming as snail mails. Good to hear from you."

It took off from there. Wes was a physically active person, seventy years old, living in the Harrisburg area. We soon were sharing phone calls with ease. He was planning on a trip to see his daughter in Ohio and wanted to stop here for an overnight. Great idea.

He sent me an email a couple days prior to the meeting. "I need to explain something to you." (That sounded like words I didn't want to hear!) "Because of my interest in skiing, mountain climbing, sailing, etc., if I put my real age in my profile I would not get active women in response, just old ladies who have taken to the couch. I am really eighty-one. I hope that you can accept this and that we can continue a promising relationship. When I call you tonight, if you want to slam down the phone I'll understand."

I took his call that evening and said, "Your age is not a turnoff, but your misrepresentation is. If you lie about this, what else may be untruthful?" I canceled our plans to meet, wishing him well.

His next and last email to me included a picture that he must have taken of himself. He was partially robed with his erect penis commandingly pointing east. "This is what you will be missing, my dear, perhaps you will want to reconsider."

I don't think so! I later saw that he had changed his age in his profile to seventy-four. Is that less of a lie? This is a lesson to all that the truth will come out sooner or later. Why bother lying?

Reward

One of the reasons you keep on with this challenging quest showed up next. His name was Sam. He had been raised in an orphanage managed by a group of German nuns who provided a strict and meager existence. Our emails from the start were very detailed, and we allowed each to enter the other's world. I had never known anyone raised in an orphanage. I was fascinated by his tales of early childhood: the single orange at Christmas, visitation by some distant family members to those around him, with no one coming to visit him. Sneaking into the kitchen at night to steal a handful of cereal. Wetting his pants in choir rehearsal because the director did not believe him when he requested to leave the room.

The top nun-in-command had some ferns in the day room that were her prized indulgence. Each day, she watered them and changed their sun direction, encouraged and admired them. Sam saw this and wished that she would extend the same caring attention to her charges. One night, he tiptoed into the day room and peed on the ferns. Imagine the dismay over the next few days as the Mother Superior watched her beloved plants turn brown. Imagine the delight it brought to one little boy locked into a dispiriting, dismal world.

Sam went on to work himself through graduate school and become head of a division of home care for the elderly that spread over several states. He was highly successful, he married, raised a family, and was later widowed. We thoroughly enjoyed our glass-of-wine telephone dates. There was always something more to discuss. Was this the perfect match? Unfortunately, Sam took in dogs creating his own form of "orphanage." He could not travel to meet anyone because there was no one to take care of the dogs the way in which he could. What a shame. In the end, he was consigned to pairing with someone very close to home, and I could only wish him the best. I really should contact him to see how he is doing.

Remorse

Step up to the plate, Hank. Here was a fellow just twenty minutes from my home. Intelligent, good

looking, kind, financially independent, educated—
the "perfect match" clues were all there. Whoops! His
marital status was legally separated. Tragically, Hank's
wife had Alzheimer's. He cared for her at home with
help coming in for several years. When her safety was
at risk, he moved her to a nursing home. For me, he
was the ideal friend. I was never sure that I wanted to
remarry, so here was a safe territory: someone who
could make no commitment demands. We actually
spent a couple years enjoying time together, going
places and doing fun activities, but there were times I
felt frustrated because here was a perfect match who
was still commited to marriage with his infirmed wife.
I went back to the keyboard for my usual outlet of
poetic expression.

Hankering
A surface love is shallow, not embracing the soul,
Giving time and energy strictly on the dole;
Half a heart in sharing, holding back the whole,
Full of dreamlike running, short of reaching any goal.

To feel a full contentment, with a freedom of display,
Needs one who is permitted to be near and wants
to stay
With unlimited times together, not just part of a day.
"Send me an unencumbered soul" becomes the
prayer I pray.
March 23, 2008

Although my heart wanted to stay right there with Hank, I never stopped seeing other men, continuing my search for the completely "right one."

Lessons Learned

Fred never should have happened. He wasn't the all-in-all that I was looking for. (I should have questioned smoking in an early phone conversation.) I was not careful enough with my "must have" list. That list should start before your first search and continue as you refine and add to it, knowing that somewhere out there, you will find the correct match. That list will grow as you read more profiles.

Some are not totally honest in their profile sketches. I learned to verbally question the items that were of great importance to me (such as smoking).

The rejection by Charlie was one that most of us have faced. We all know the feeling. The danger is that it can halt further searching. Risk is involved at any level of a relationship, and building trust takes time. Perhaps a limit of miles would have been wise, as we lived in two different worlds. I then put that on my list: western Pennsylvania or eastern Ohio. It was imperative to keep moving. Hearts do heal.

Poor Sam had so much to offer, but I think that his past caught up with him. Taking in orphans was his quest, this time with homeless hounds—what fortunate dogs they were. I often wonder if he found "the girl next door." I look back at the importance of coupling even for a while with another person. Opening up memories in honest conversation and sharing dreams are important when you've been single and not sharing those thoughts. Thank you, Sam.

And Wes—what can I say? There will be men out there who will be dishonest about their age. The more you talk before meeting them, the better your chances at catching lies in their profile. Try this question thrown unexpectedly into a conversation: "What year were you born?" Any hesitation is telling! We all know the year we were born without hesitation. He was a poor loser, as evidenced by his final attempt with the picture of his "endowment." You'll run into them.

Everyone should have a "Hank." There's nothing like a steady, loving friend through all the moving around from one prospect to another. He was an anchor for sanity in my whirlwind world of Internet dating. He will always remain a very special friend.

Chapter 4—Rob Comes Back to the Drawing Board

Encore

Hello again. Over a year has passed since my first exposure to Internet dating. As you might remember, it resulted in a wonderful year-long relationship with the playwright. We parted friends, and I was confident that it was not the end of the world. Why? Because the world of Internet dating was just a click away. Now I was experienced in its ways, or so I thought.

Refinement

My playwright friend and I had compared Internet dating experiences, which brought additional insights for us both. Being in my midsixties, I decided that this time I would try a dating service (or services) that catered to the more mature crowd. I signed up with Senior Singles.

I updated my profile, uploaded my picture, narrowed my age preference from sixty to seventy years old, and specified a twenty-mile radius. I clicked and waited. Wow . . . I was inundated. Wait a minute. This one was from the West Coast, this one was from the East Coast. More and more were from down state. Only two were within the twenty mile area I had specified. I went back and reviewed my preferences, concentrating on the twenty mile radius. Same thing again. Fortunately, I had signed up for only three months.

I complained to the site managers that they were not honoring my request in terms of age and distance. When I tried to cancel I got the runaround. Their response to my first complaint was a form letter. It did not touch on my specific issues but said that I should "investigate" every respondent to find the right one. Their next response advised that all members nationwide could see my listing and emphasized the advantage of unlimited choices. In several other frustrating exchanges, they took the position that their service was providing superior benefits and advantages. They suggested that I was not using their service to its full potential. Oh yeah? How about using their promise of a radius filter for starters? I was getting inquiries from all over the country. This site is not in business today. I wonder why!

Discoveries

I learned quickly that not all Internet dating services are the same in terms of quality and ethics.

As I became more experienced and tried various services, I found most sites list a lot of members who had not renewed their membership and therefore couldn't respond. They were no longer active for whatever reason (hopefully because they found somebody and were not disappointed by an unfortunate coupling). This is a major fault of the dating services. They should display only active members. Some sites deliberately list defunct members to make their numbers appear impressively larger. Beware of the sites that have excessive numbers of nonactive memberships. Don't waste your energy on candidates who are listed as inactive for over three months.

I went back to one of the larger Internet services, Match.com. When registering, I did not upload my photo. I had shaved my beard of thirty some years and needed a new photo, but I was anxious to get back into dating, so I went ahead without the photo. This service had many listings within my twenty-mile radius preference, so many that I contacted only those women with an appealing photo and an interesting profile. (I knew I should be looking for the inner beauty, but I had to start somewhere.) I received several inquiries and a few flirts from ladies, but most contacts happened because I made the initial move. My new photo without the beard wasn't ready, and photos do make a difference!

One on One

About a dozen contacts progressed to nice email exchanges over the next several weeks. It was time for the next big step: the coffee date. Over the next month or so, I had an average of one or two coffee dates a week. I want to state that every lady I met in this series and subsequently over the years treated me with utmost respect and kindness in these face-to-face "preliminaries," as I think I did in return. From what I hear, not all men do. It makes you wonder how many nice friendships are missed.

I tried to prepare for each meeting by reminding myself of an interest or item they had mentioned in their email or a question about their community. This tactic was not very original, but once the ice was broken and the normal first-time meeting tensions alleviated, conversations usually flowed. I had to be careful not to slip into mentioning memories and experiences that had involved my late wife.

This phase of Internet dating was like Basic Training for me. I learned that the ladies I met that I wanted to see more of didn't want to see more of *me*. The ones that really didn't interest me didn't want to close the door. I think the reason for this was that the ladies I liked had been out in the world and had careers most of their lives. They were used to making decisions on their own, and they knew what they wanted. The ones that didn't reject me (although none were pleading for my undivided attention) had been homemakers most of their lives and now, because of divorce or widowhood, were finding themselves on their own for the first time. They were not quite sure what they wanted or how to find that out through Internet dating. They were exploring, hoping for the best. Perhaps the difference in older relationship dynamics, based on the work/marriage backgrounds we bring to the coffee date, is a book in itself.

I slowly began to realize that a) I didn't know what *I* wanted and b) I better learn to communicate rather than pontificate. It was ironic that a retired ad man whose lifetime business was communication realized that he had to learn to communicate on a personal level. Not so ironic was a guy realizing that he had to learn not to talk like the *decision maker center-of-the-universe* model he (and most men) lived by his entire life. Perhaps it is women's fault that guys are so egotistical and self-centered! You brought us into this world, mothered us, sought us out as mates, told us how wonderful we were, forgave us when we strayed and/or failed, caressed our bodies, massaged our egos, and deferred to our lame-brained decisions. Who wouldn't be more than a little spoiled and exactly what ladies don't want to deal with in the last and best years of their lives? Talk about irony! Maybe that's also another book.

On-Site Training

During these first contacts, there were a lot of learning experiences, such as the music professor at a local college with whom I had a delightful lunch and walk. I wanted to see her again. She cordially said that I was a nice, interesting person but "no thank you." This was a very straightforward lady. She was pleasant and seemed to want to express her reasons for the rejection: to allay my hurt and her conscience. She said that there just wasn't any "chemistry" for her, so why should we waste each others' time. It wasn't me, and it really wasn't her. Her clear-eyed, no-fault take on the matter was refreshing and an important lesson. In the future, such total honesty when properly delivered put the dating scene for me, and consequently my contacts, on a much higher level.

There was a wealthy lady whose high-profile lawyer husband had passed suddenly ten years earlier. She lived in a spectacular mansion with a huge in-ground swimming pool. I believe she had not dated since her husband's death; I think her friends had an intervention with her about getting back into circulation, dating-wise, and I was probably her first date. I took her out to the theater, several concerts, and for some fine dining. However, every time I came to pick her up for the evening, she had just finished the day with her numerous grandchildren at her pool. She couldn't stop talking about her grandchildren for the entire evening. Every evening. I had enough after four or five dates and decided to move on.

Don't bring too much family "baggage" to the dating scene. Baggage includes too much history of past relationships. I couldn't avoid the wealthy woman's baggage, but it made me aware that I was doing the same thing in talking about my late wife way too much. It is hard to spend over 50 percent of your life experiences with someone and not have those memories slip into conversations, but for everyone's sake, keep it minimal! It is a real turnoff and a turn down to the other person. This was another lesson learned: I'm trying to build *new* relationships, not relive past ones.

Each coffee date was an adventure. I was learning, and I found that the people across the table were also in various levels of their learning experiences.

One was an interior designer. I wanted to be an architect when I was young, and we were able to exchange a lot of interesting trade talk. I was hoping that I had met my match until she let it be known that she didn't have any designs on me. Lesson learned: Rejection is a living, breathing monster on the dating scene. Be ready for it.

Then there was the college administrator. We shared a love of classical music. She would never invite me into her home because of her dogs. I never knew how many she actually had, but in looking in her front bay window, I could see that she had stretched sheets over the entire living room carpeting and presumably throughout the house. Weren't the dogs housebroken? (I certainly was.) After several dates, I realized that I couldn't compete with the dogs. One wrong step in this relationship, and I pictured an overnight "in the doghouse," and winter was coming. I moved on before the dogs nipped at my heels.

Reconnoiter

Frankly, I was becoming a little concerned. I thought that my conversational skills were improving—I was minimizing talk about the wife and family baggage. I was learning that I really like women and talking to them. For me, that was a revelation.

I really had not found a woman that wanted me or one that I wanted. There was no match in the making with Match.com. I hoped that a photo would improve the situation, because I was becoming disillusioned with my dating life via the Internet. I was now occasionally making contacts only by sending an occasional flirt.

Bingo!

One day, a lady responded who lived only several miles away in the next suburb. We emailed back and forth until it seemed like it was the right time for the coffee date. Remember, she had not seen a picture of me, but I had seen one of her. Because it was my birthday and I was feeling lonely, instead of a coffee date, I suggested a nice dinner at my favorite restaurant. She accepted. We looked forward to a nice dinner and time together. As it unfolded, this date was simply amazing! You would have become a believer in some sort of predestination of life. Very early in the dinner, we found out that her phone number was only one digit different than mine! Then we found out that we had mutual friends—actually, two groups of mutual friends and intertwining work and social connections beyond belief. It was amazing that we hadn't crossed paths previously. That's how I met Julia. I learned that Internet dating does work, if you're persistent, patient, and willing to learn and adapt.

Julia and I lived, loved, and traveled together for more than three wonderful years. I dropped my Internet dating subscription, and that should have been the "they lived happily ever after."

Devastation

Wrong. One day Julia called me and simply stated that she didn't want to see me anymore. I didn't see this coming in the slightest. We had no arguments or seeming dissatisfaction. She assured me that it wasn't another man. We were of different faiths, but neither one of us was very religious, and so that was never an issue. The parting was civil, but to this day, I only have theories of why Julia changed her mind about me. Was I not attentive to her intellectual needs? Was it religious pressure from family members? Was it another man? I probably will never know. The important thing was to put it behind me and move on as quickly as I could. Internet dating allows you to do this better than anything I know.

However, I did not take the loss well at all. I was devastated. Kubler-Ross's Five Stages of Grief include Denial, Anger, Bargaining, Depression and Acceptance. I went through all those emotions in a period of several months. In my case, before Acceptance, I added *Rage*. I was furious. Eventually, I realized that I needed to get back into Internet dating so that *Rage* would not be followed by Revenge. I'm not as nice a person as you might have suspected.

Reprise

Once again, I went back to Internet dating services. I joined two: one old, Match.com, and one new, Seniormatch.com. I was going to approach Internet dating like I would approach the market for one of my advertising clients, only this time I was the client. (I know the old saying about not being your own lawyer, and it's probably true here for me, but I didn't know any professional match makers.) I wanted numbers of contacts, and I was willing to work for them. I started to make contact with every woman registered in these two services within twenty miles, sometimes with just a flirt, sometimes with a personalized note. I kept files on who responded and what they said. I ranked them by a system I developed of my preferences and their interest in me. To my pleasant surprise, I also contacted ladies who did not have a picture with their profile. This was a literal treasure trove! Because they didn't have a picture, they received fewer responses, so in contacting them, I had less competition. They seemed more—how shall I say it?—"responsive." I was spending two to four hours a day emailing back and forth with all these ladies. Being busy in itself helped to ease my hurt and anger from being dumped unexpectedly by Julia. In this phase, I discovered that I really liked women. I liked their attitude and flexibility and humanity about this stage of our lives. Most of my male friends wanted to relive their past careers or many were just plain checking out, both mentally and too often in their daily lives. Four of my long-time male friends died within eighteen months during this period. Many of the ladies from this period became great pen pals, and a few remain so to this day, years later.

I had a ballooning file of area ladies to meet, and meet them I did. My system was to meet them for coffee first. Then, if there was some mutual interest, I invited them for a dinner and/or movie. You ladies reading this may think my system was too methodical and cold—perhaps, but it assured me that I would have a lot more ladies in my life, and I wasn't missing the one that could make all the difference.

As pleased as I was with this approach, let me assure you, it was work! For several months I averaged seven to nine coffee dates and up to three dinner and movie dates a week, plus there were several hours daily of emails! Fortunately, I'm retired and had the time. There was a time that, without keeping files, I would have missed dates, had people and profiles all jumbled, and made a fool of myself in front of the very ladies I wanted to impress and know better.

Payday

In these months, I met a lot of interesting women. Some liked me, and some couldn't care less, but I think my experiences gave me the ability to better appreciate, evaluate, converse, and respond to women than ever before in my life. I think we all benefited from the experiences.

One lady who had a business of restoring antique homes was impressed with my real estate marketing skills. First, she tried to use our dates for marketing consultation. Then she wanted to hire my professional services. My intent was to build a personal relationship, not a professional one.

Another was an aspiring poet who was only interested in my knowledge of the publishing business. Another liked to travel and made this clear: no travel, no relationship. Fair enough. I hope she finds someone. Actually, I travel a fair amount, but not under her restrictive conditions. She wanted to pick the locations and be the pretty eye candy on my arm. No thank you.

Another could speak a half-dozen languages. On our coffee date, she lapsed into talking like the character Nastasha in the "Rocky and Bullwinkle" cartoons. She was funny and broke me up when she went into the Nastasha personality. I thought she was going to be great. On our second date for dinner, we were having a super time until while walking in a park she asked me if I would like to come home with her and tie her up in the basement for a little bondage play. She wasn't kidding. I'm not one to make judgment on such matters, but she was moving too fast for me and my preferences. I believe I was being lured to her house for blackmail purposes or worse. This is a reminder of the need to be cautious when making contact with the strangers you meet in your Internet dating. Always keep alert. Not all out there are what they seem to be.

Over that year, I narrowed it down to several relationships. They all know that I do not want to get married again, and they say that they do not see marriage again for themselves. Interestingly, those feeling this way are split between career ladies and former homemakers. In several instances, several of us socialize together. It is the way life should be at this time in our lives.

All in all, Internet dating has made my golden years truly golden. It has introduced me to places, pleasures, and people I never dreamed of. Wonderful people.

Lessons Learned
Beware of Internet dating services that do not stay within the parameters you specify, like location. Don't use services that continue to list expired memberships. Do not bother contacting people who have not been active for three months or more.

Treat all coffee dates and inquiries with respect. Reply to all flirts and correspondence. Be honest and straightforward. Not all will show you the same courtesy, but the positives will be in your favor, and you'll feel better about yourself.

Leave the personal baggage at home. Keep information on grandchildren, past marriages, and relationships to the minimum. Remember that you're online and meeting these new people to build a future, not to dwell in the past.

Know what you're looking for in a relationship. This is not easy and will change as your experiences grow. Don't be too limited. Have some guidelines so that you don't waste your time and others' time.

Never, never become despondent in the process. The next one might be THE one, and it only takes one to make your life very, very complete.

Contact a lot of potential dates. This practice will help you be ready to know when the right one comes along, and you'll make a lot of new friends in the process.

Be vigilant. You are dealing with total strangers. There's a reason they're called strangers—some are really strange! Always meet in safe, public places until you are absolutely certain about them.

Chapter 5—Off We Go

The Male Perspective

Wasn't that last chapter an eye opener for women of my age who thought men were the controllers of the destiny of love? They initiated the phone calls. They were the ones asking for dates. They were the ones proposing marriage. You can see from Rob's writing that his heart was broken. He went through the necessary learning and sorting in his romantic pilgrimage, and you have now seen that there is struggle on both sides. We will go on to see if it is worth it.

All Aboard

As you travel this dating road with me, tighten your seatbelt. It gets bumpy. It has infinite highs and bottomless lows, but travel we must. I am an overachiever, and I had committed myself to this quest. I would see it to the end. But what end? Would you believe that I had no defined ending? Marriage? Companionship? Pen pals? Casual or *un*casual dating?

Every day was dedicated to a little more exposure to Internet dating. To make sure that I didn't miss anyone, I joined five services—yes, five—with a different user name on each and altered but honest profiles. I was surprised at the number of men who covered all the bases in the same way. There were several times when I got overtures from the same person but from a different site.

Local Tour

Nothing was quite so exciting as to see a local candidate with appealing details in his profile. Let me tell you the story about Ben who lived just a few miles away, which is always an advantage over a long distance one. Let's listen in on this little soap opera.

He wrote very well . . . could actually spell, not common even in many educated men. Full of vitality . . . loved spontaneous adventure . . . into many fun activities like golfing and fishing. One big negative: he had had a stroke, which caused him to use a cane. Claimed it did not slow down his activity level and that he was diligently following the recommended therapy. Sad because he was only sixty-three years old. She liked them a little younger because of her energy level, but this was a little extreme. Check it out. Maybe not.

She looked good, really good. Stunning black-and-white outfit topped by a good hair day. She was extremely curious about this one.

She arrived at the restaurant and entered the bar as planned. He flashed a warm smile on his handsome face and gave a wave , putting her immediately at ease. He was on the second half of a beer.

"Wanna stay here and have a drink or go to a table?"

"Table." She was not about to get into a lengthy bar scene on an empty stomach. She headed to the door to the dining room, stopping at the entrance to see whether he preferred a table or booth. Turning, she saw that this poor fellow had traveled only four feet from where he started. The movement was obviously painful, the look on his face more so. She stifled her immediate

"pity response." This was an exploring adventure, not a caregiver outing.

Finally at the table, conversation was not difficult. He had had an interesting career life from hotel management to owning his own trucking company. He dropped teasers about his many travels, a deluxe motor home and boat. Teasers that for her had long since faded in their impressive strength. Just get to the person, stripped of material amenities!

Midway in what could have been an acceptable happening, he admitted that he was seventy years old (at that point, she would have guessed seventy-four). A discussion of "truth" in profiles followed. She shared the story of one who had lied about his age. "It wasn't the true age that disturbed me, it was the lying. I dropped him without a meeting." If he caught her innuendo, he disguised it well.

Then the clincher, the magical moment that screamed "turnoff!" Although he had a minimal potbelly, the button covering his belly button opened, exposing a hairy belly to a woman who had not been intimate with bellies full of hair for many years. Amidst the hair was a pink scar line straight down the middle, inferring a surgery that she had no interest in discussing. She found it a challenge to take in all this information using quick, sweeping eye gestures rather than staring. She felt no obligation to tell him to button up, as somehow that seemed too intimate a request for the occasion.

When he asked about the career choices of her two husbands, she answered, "One was an engineer, the other a family physician." She could see him recoil. This was a real important moment, when he saw the unlikely match. Now he could suggest, "I really enjoyed our time together, but I'm not sure I find in you the qualities that I seek." He could leave without suffering rejection.

All in all, he had enjoyed not only her company but another beer and two vodka tonics. Perhaps they were poor choices for someone who already had a walking problem.

They parted with the usual "Best to you, and I hope you find the right person." She ran to her car feeling the joy of escape, the satisfaction of singleness, the appeal of independence! She loved the pick-and-choose advantage that Internet dating provided. So many choices. Some would be good, others not so good, but as she traveled the dating road, she knew those choices could improve one step at a time.

Beyond the Fold of the Map

Maybe it's a mistake to limit oneself to the local area. You might venture just a little further, as the grass may truly be greener.

Kevin lived beside a lake in Ohio about two hours from me. He was retired but still occupied with restoring antique cars. His work shed was a treasure house of tools that he gladly shared with neighbors (as long as they signed a posted sheet so that he knew where the tools were if he needed them). He was an obviously kind man with a quiet charm so often found in a shy person. He wrote, "I'll be in your area to check out a '56 Chevie next week. Love to check you out also." We set a date for lunch.

He was tall, a little over six foot, and quick to smile. The lunch talk was about families and lost loves. We had both shared in the loss of spouse. I guess widowers were my weakness—the passage of time left them with such fond memories of their wives. (Many of the divorced men had that chip splintering their shoulders. I didn't want to pay for another woman's acts of unkindness!)

Kevin and I left the restaurant and took a long, leisurely walk in the park by the river. We sat on a waterfront bench and watched trains and boats, imagining exotic destinations. It was so comfortable being with him. After a quiet time on that bench he said, "I think we could have something going here. I want to see you again. Why don't you drive out to see my place. It's beautiful on the lake.

We could even do some fishing." Bingo! Magic words.

The next couple weeks were filled with email and phone calls planning my visit. It was close enough that I could make it a round trip all in one day. On a sunny Tuesday morning, I set out to see this wonderful place by the lake with its welcoming home and the productive work shed in back. It was easy to find, and I pulled into a long driveway that led toward the lake. And there it was: little more than a shack, maybe two rooms plus a bath. The productive shed was a worn lean-to. I wanted to turn around, but Kevin had been such a dear person that I could not. He greeted me with a big hug and spent the day hosting with fishing, food, and more warm conversation. Later in the day I told him

I was a city girl, just not suited for isolated living, but I would love to stay in touch. ("Stay in touch" meant slowly withdrawing the communication. Dating world regulars understand that.) By early evening, I headed down the road, a little sorry that I could not be the person Kevin needed and wanted so much. I often wonder if he ever found her.

Shoulda Called AAA

Each morning I went to the computer to see who was online. Who had sent a flirt or a message? Had I received a response from yesterday's correspondence? The gurus behind the scene at the sites encourage you to send messages, not just flirts. You can check to see who has looked at your profile, and sometimes that's a nice lead for sending a message.

Slippery Road

Pack up, here we go. Leonard had checked my profile three times over the period of a week without sending a flirt or a message. He was seventy-one, six foot one, blue eyes, balding white hair, had owned a publishing company, and now lived in a retirement community not far from me. I sent him a message asking if he was too shy to write. "I promise to treat you gently and to respond to you if you write a little about yourself. What's the harm?" Two days went by, and then, there he was—a lengthy message about his lifestyle and his need for companionship, an admission that some men seem to find difficult. I found it charming. And yes, he was a shy person. I knew I would have to play the aggressor. After several more emails, I suggested that we talk on the phone: "Writing is a great start, but it lacks eye contact, voice inflection, and meaningful pauses. And laughter." I gave him my cell phone number (a safer move than the land line which could be traced—always moving with caution).

What a fun person! We laughed our way through that first conversation. He made up for any lack due to shyness with quick repartee. Leonard had nursed his wife through Alzheimer's disease, putting his life on hold. Since her death and a required time of grieving, he was ready to resume a full life. Several weeks went by as we enjoyed call after call. It was time to arrange a meeting and I was really anticipating this one.

We were talking about the effect the Great Depression had on our parents. I told him, "My father would hang up a paper towel after drying his hands. He figured that his hands were clean when he used it, therefore it was clean enough for further use." He said, "My mother boiled every bone in sight for nutritious broth. I was a teenager before I found out you could buy soup in a can!"

Then I asked, "What year were you born?" The "1926" was blurted out uncensored. He was eighty-two, ten years my senior and too many to be practical. I did not want to promote an opportunity to be widowed again. He pleaded for my understanding but, again, the lying was paramount in my judgment of him. With sadness, I said "Goodbye, Leonard."

Traffic Jam

I was really looking forward to meeting Glenn. He wrote, "I treasured my years with my wife. As a minister and lecturer on marital relationships, I thanked God every day for Rita. We were truly the classic 'soul mates.' I'm ready to duplicate those pleasurable years." Okay, it sounded like a winner as long as I didn't have to be "Rita." After the necessary correspondence by computer and phone, we planned a dinner meeting here in town. What a refreshing person he was! As we savored stuffed pork chops, I discovered that he was totally into my criteria for an exemplary relationship. Because he was a minister, I felt comfortable inviting him back to the house for a decadent piece of home-made pecan pie.

As I was preparing our treat, he came from behind and grabbed, fondled, and turned me around to unsuccessfully slobber around the area of my mouth. What an unexpected and unwelcome display of horniness. As I pulled away, he admitted, "Rita has only been gone a month, and I miss our sexual activity. She was so perfect in expressing herself and how she felt about me."

There it was. I had an opportunity to be Rita in case I was tired of being myself. No thank you. Before he could enjoy the pecan pie, I showed him to the door and out of my life. I should have inquired about the date of Rita's death before I planned to meet him. There was no way that I would subject myself to a man who was deeply mourning, abandoned, and looking for a replacement. I learned a lesson: there's room for only one girl on my road!

Rest Stop

Each morning, I revisited the sites to check new messages and to see who had viewed me. I also checked the new listings in my area. This took about an hour, sometimes longer if I was writing emails of any length. When friends openly envied my dating, they had no idea that it was a part-time job to pursue these opportunities. "Make It Happen" was time consuming and tedious, but it included the anticipation of finding that right person. I enjoyed the interesting encounters with the rejects that I lovingly referred to as my "frogs." It was a delightful hobby for the "people person" that I am, and because I am an overachiever, I never stop until a goal is accomplished. There was a constant overlap of prospects, and my friends wondered how I kept them all straight. "What if two show up at the same time?" Fortunately, I never had to face that dilemma.

One Way

You know you're caught on a one-way street when no one else is going your way. You think you're right, but the fellow going the other direction knows he's the one who is right and in total control. He can pull your strings the right way and then cut those strings, dropping you to a useless heap on the Internet dating ground. Acceptance and rejection are two mighty forces battling their way through Internet Dating Land. Acceptance is delightful. The return of the first attempt at correspondence, the daily email from someone special, and the plans to meet are all positive and welcome. Rejection is tough at any level in the process of getting acquainted. Be prepared for it and handle it. Rejection can be the best thing to happen to you if the match is not right.

A humiliating rejection episode that comes to mind involved a really appealing fellow named Scott. For several weeks, we had been in touch every other day, and he lived nearby. The Fourth of July was imminent, and Scott was alone in the city. When he asked me on the phone, "What are you doing on the Fourth?" I admitted, "No plans." His voice perked up, "Well, let's have our own picnic. I'll bring the food. You do the hardware." I offered my place, knowing that I would be more comfortable on my own territory.

On the third of July, he called me with his menu. "You'll love my potato salad. Secret ingredients. Cold cuts and buns. I wasn't sure whether you had a grill. And I baked my grandmother's favorite chocolate cake. You don't mind if it doesn't have frosting, do you? I'm not that good a cook."

"No frosting is fine with me," I answered, "that's more calories left for the potato salad!"

That evening, I got out the dishes and flatware. I put condiments in lovely serving dishes, selected some wine, and looked forward to the next day.

Scott planned to arrive at high noon. At one o'clock, there still was no Scott. I tried calling. No answer. For several hours, I called on the hour with no answer.

I sent an email, "What happened?"

I never heard from Scott again. I did send another email: "You had every right to change your mind, but no right to treat me as you did. Your profile stated that you 'knew how to treat a lady.' Obviously you do not. Please do not write or call me." That tag on the end helped me feel some control in reaction to his rudeness. At last check, he was still on the site.

Poor Navigation

I decided to put down the map and travel forward without a second thought of my destination and what might be waiting there. Forget about the "distance thing"—get carried away with day dreams.

Mark was a creative designer of movie theaters, the kind in the large complexes with many choices under one roof. He traveled a lot to supervise on-site construction, and he was full of interesting travel stories. I don't know that I would ever want an "on the road" kind of job, but it sure did sound interesting when someone else told the story. He had met real movie stars, survived a small plane crash in Iowa, and had stayed in a hotel with bed bugs.

After six weeks of sharing through emails and phone conversations Mark asked me to come for a visit. He was in the midst of a job that demanded his staying at home in Dunkirk, New York. That was just far enough away for me to feel the wanderlust inspired by his tales. I made reservations for myself at a motel in Dunkirk. I was really feeling grown up, woman of the worldish, heading out on another great adventure.

It was one of those storybook October days when the sun made the colors of the leaves vibrant. It was a nice day to travel north to meet this highly successful, wealthy, handsome man about town. I wasn't sure that there was any promise of a lasting relationship. This was more of an adventure, a tale for a winter's eve. I pulled up in front of a $659,000 home (a figure he just happened to work into a conversation) in a plush neighborhood. I had just called him on my cell phone, so he was standing in the door waiting for me. How romantic! With a nice hug, he said, "Come on in!"

I'm not sure I can adequately describe the opulence of the interior. Every piece of furniture looked like a featured "piece of the week" in a home décor magazine. The living room was two stories high with an overhang balcony around it. The library looked like it was taken from a Lionel Barrymore film of the 1940s. It was breathtaking, and so was he. It was near noon, so he invited me to go to a local restaurant, not a chain, for one of those "everything you've always wanted in a salad" salads. Conversation was easy—it was just listening to his adventures. We then headed to see a movie, "George W," watched it, and gave it four stars.

We headed back to the house. Mark was into cultural activities, so I was sure he had planned dinner and a play, opera, symphony, or whatever for the evening. We sat at the kitchen table comparing the print-outs of our profiles. He then suggested, "Let's put a DVD on in the bedroom and diddle a while."

I'm not sure of the exact definition of "diddle," but I was sure it was not in my guidebook of recommended first-date activities. I suggested instead that I needed to check in at the motel to secure my room. When he called later, I explained that for me intimacy was saved for much later in a relationship when commitment was expressed. So marked the end of Mark.

Head-on Crash

Back to the map. An attractive, direct roadway on the map can be deceiving, as deceiving as some profiles such as this one:

"Although I am quite close with my four children (even though they are scattered throughout the country), I truly miss the comforting presence of a special woman. Oh yes, I've dated during the past four years that I've been widowed, but that reaction called 'chemistry' just hasn't happened. I want an independent woman who chooses to be with me. A woman who can speak her own mind but who can also compromise when necessary in a loving relationship. I'm finding women who are either grossly independent (and I wonder why they are even pursuing a relationship), or they are spineless and uninteresting as if they are counting on a man to give them some worthwhile identity. I'm not perfect, but I will do everything to find the 'perfect' coupling."

Who wouldn't want to be that special woman? I would guess that many of us strive to be flexibly independent, turning it on or off as necessary. My profile described the "right man who will instinctively know when to give me my independent moments and when to be close for comfort and sharing."

I wrote to the profile owner: "Hi, Dan, it certainly registered a direct hit when I read your profile. And why shouldn't you spell it out so that all the window shoppers know whether to stop in or move on? This one is stopping me. I would like to get to know you. Please refer to my profile for some matching thoughts. On the Avenue."

I waited a day. Then there he was! He wanted to send me a picture, if I cared to give my personal email address. Just to be safe, I wrote back that I would appreciate speaking to him first. Would he please send a phone number? He did.

"Hi, Dan. On the Avenue calling."

" Hi there, On the Avenue. How's it going?"

"It's going fine. Nice to hear your voice. You indicated South Side Pittsburgh as home. Is that really South Side or some other community in that direction?"

"Actually, it's Mt. Lebanon. I've lived here for thirty years after a transfer from Baltimore."

"My mother was from Baltimore. I spent many childhood vacations there visiting family.

Nice city."

There was a slight pause, and then he asked, "Would you want to live there?"

"No, I'm nicely rooted here. I even enjoy snowy winters."

"I like your voice and I like your picture, I sure would like to meet you. I'll email you a picture and you can decide whether you like cross-eyed men!"

"Don't get too excited! My picture doesn't reveal my bowed legs!"

"I'll bet they are beautiful legs, legs that I would love to have wrapped around me in a sweaty passionate embrace, your beautiful bare breasts pressed against my bare body as you scream for more. A man has needs, you know."

I was speechless, shaken, and disappointed. I had endured a "screen rape" and now a "phone rape." I slammed down the phone in shock and sat there, stunned. This was so far removed from what I had expected. The need to fight back began to fill my thoughts. I was glad I never gave him my first name. Ha ha! I used my cell phone, so he couldn't trace me. I thought, I should wrap my legs around his neck in a stranglehold until he screams for mercy. "A man has needs?" Well, his needs will never be filled by me! Even his voice turned me off. Thank God he was faceless!

That was the end of Dan.

Stop to Refill

I took a deep breath and remembered my mission to Make It Happen. Mustn't be stopped by roadblocks! Time to move on. I was getting more seasoned at this game. Each time a lesson was learned, and each time, I went back to the computer with a positive anticipation that the next time would be different. The Right One would soon be galloping in on his horse to whisk me off into Loveland.

On and On, Again and Again

Sometimes I question "Make It Happen."
A feasible reality or a foolish dream?
Am I tethered to an illusionary goal,
A teasing brass ring, a sneering scheme?

These unknown men I now pursue
Are not as I would have them be.
They misrepresent with pictures and words
Fooling themselves or just fooling me?

To Make It Happen requires fortitude
A willingness to try and then try again.
Somewhere out there he's ready for me;
I just don't know the where or the when.

Right Turn

Jim had the potential for being The Right One. A sports writer for a large newspaper in Ohio, he was a rare combination of creative and jock. He had studied theater in college along with journalism while he played end on the football team. We wrote lengthy emails back and forth expressing our views, agreeable or not. I loved his sense of humor, and it motivated me to write well in response to him. He still did some freelance writing but kept a light schedule in favor of being on the road unencumbered. After experiencing the anguish of a second divorce, he sold his home and bought a motor home. Now his main writing itch was to put together a collection of short "on the road" experiences, publish them in book form, and live comfortably the rest of his life on the millions the book earned for him. I read some of the writings, and they were delightfully descriptive.

In the midst of the quick turnover acquaintances offered by Internet dating, you are sometimes blessed with a special person, and Jim was certainly that one in a million. We spent three September days together, and it was like having my dearly loved brother back again. On our first meeting, he came to my door with dark glasses on and portrayed a "blind date." It was not offensive, it was hilarious, and so started a fun time together. I never felt that Jim and I were to have a romance, as our relationship was on a totally different level. We teased sexually, but we never engaged in anything other than a genuine hug and a quick kiss on the cheek. We did some sightseeing around Pittsburgh. We played golf, delighted that we were equally lousy, one more thing in common. We shopped and we cooked. It all came so naturally, so effortlessly with him. I admired the freedom of his lifestyle but knew I could never share it—that city girl thing again. I was sad to see him go, wishing him well, not knowing if we would meet again but knowing that we would stay in touch, and we have.

A typical exchange from Jim occurred the following Christmas. I wrote to him to say, "The wheels of Christmas are spinning. This will be my third night in a row of Christmas dinner out with friends, a break on Sunday, Monday they start again. (Don't eat the rolls, no potato, don't order dessert, schedule an extra stop at the gym—these thoughts played over and over in my head.)

All the presents are under my tree, can't wait to see the family dig in. Still have to bake a few more expected cookies. Where will you spend Christmas? Do I have to worry about you being alone, sobbing over Christmas Past?"

Jim answered, "I'm all alone for Christmas. I bought some frozen White Castle hamburgers which I may eat as is or possibly heat in the microwave. This will be my dinner along with some milk (only slightly soured).

I heard they're crying for me in Argentina. No gifts, but at least I got a card. It was from my insurance agent, and he offered me a good deal on a premium rate for Christmas.

After I eat my White Castle, I may go down to the Mission for dessert and possibly a gift for us broken-down old timers who defended our country during war times. Maybe I'll get another pair of gloves. Last year, although the left was a different color than the right one, they were the same size. Warm gloves sure do come in handy here in Florida, especially if I get a job building a snowman.

I have to go now. I got a notice that a care package is waiting for me at the Salvation Army. Jim."

How could you not love him?

Here is another of our written conversations. This came the end of December when we shared our resolutions for the new year.

Jim wrote, "Wow! This is weird. We have the same resolutions. I too am resolving to stop dieting, exercising, etc."

I answered, "Scares me to death that I have so much in common with you!"

Jim: "Without Sally around (his imaginary town whore) and no girl friend, I've stopped sex.

Thank goodness, I won't have to take those pills anymore."

Me: "Darn! You were next on my list."

Jim: "Talking about you know what, I had a new bed partner last night. She's a cute little kitty, her name is Cat. She has long hair and is extremely affectionate. I think I fell in love with her an hour after we met."

Me: "Be careful. Coughing up those hairballs can be tricky!"

Jim: "Old Friend (the girl he dumped) hasn't come to visit although she is threatening. Also, my ex-wife wants me to visit her or she would like to visit me. She told me that she loves me."

Me: "Gosh, life is really scary. Let old friends threaten. You know better than to learn a lesson twice. As for Sally, everyone loves you. It happens around the holidays. See how she feels on a cold dark day in January."

Jim: "I am expecting a visit from another old friend around January 8 for a week or so. I hope Cat doesn't throw me over and crawl in with him some night."

Me: "Worries me more that in your present state you may crawl in with him. Keep the lights on."

I include this later note from him because it so well portrays his playful humor.

"Today I played softball with the old timers. (Actually I think I'm the oldest.) I got a hit and grounded out twice; then I visited the dentist and got two old fillings replaced. Now I'm home, and loving Cat who is being most responsive like most females are to me. Gee, I hate being such a darn sex object!

At five thirty today, I will meet an Internet lady who looks kinda pretty and, unfortunately, will probably want sex on the first date. Well, she's going to find out she's barking up the wrong tree with me! We are meeting at a restaurant, and she said she'd be the lady with a red rose clasped between her teeth. I told her I'd be wearing a dirty t-shirt, stained and torn shorts, a frayed straw hat. I think she's a classy lady because she replied that she is pleased that I decided to dress for dinner. Anyway, I will be happy to get home and go to bed with my new lady." (I assume and hope he means Cat.)

My New Year's greeting to him read: "My dear friend, a very Happy New Year to you. I get the feeling that you have a lot of dreams that need to come true! Marti."

Neither one of us knew how close that was to happening.

Keep Your Eyes on the Road

As we travel, we must watch for bumps and potholes or detours that save us from traveling dangerous highways. Always stay alert for words or actions that indicate, "Travel at your own risk."

Jerry lost his wife to divorce when his business collapsed. A marriage several years later ended the day after the wedding when Jerry discovered that his new wife had been successfully hiding her alcoholism from him.

We were in the second hour of our five-hour lunch when Jerry finished his story with, "as a result, I served three years in prison." (What!!! Wakeup words at a first lunch with a potential friend, lover, or mate!)

Jerry had been telling me about his dilemma with his former business partner. The two had a realty company. Jerry had the sales personality and Tom was the true "bean counter," content to work the numbers with the company's profits and investments. It was a perfect marriage of talents until Tom secreted himself out of town with pockets full of company and investor's money. Tom was on vacation when an investor asked Jerry to withdraw his money, and the fraud was discovered. Jerry tried to locate Tom with professional "people finders." A death certificate was found in Arizona, but Jerry never believed its veracity. The issue went to trial in front of a judge who was a personal friend of one of the investors. Jerry felt the judge heard the case but his fairness was questionable.

Jerry now had to live within court boundaries for three years. A probation officer visited him once a month to check on his progress; it was a demeaning but necessary routine.

He was back working in real estate trying to recoup some of the material possessions lost in the settlement: his home, a Cadillac, and jewelry.

He said, "This is not an easy story to tell someone on first meeting, but it's a cross I must bear in fairness to a potential mate."

He was such a bright, appealing person, and his honesty made him even more so. My mind shuddered with the uneasiness of having to explain any of that to family and friends if I were to see him again. There was an innocence in Jerry that came through in that sharing session. He brought me a bouquet of straw flowers that he had raised and dried as a hobby; they are now in an arrangement on my dining room table each autumn. They bring memories of that luncheon and of many well-written emails.

After several months, I received an email that said, "I have become acquainted with four intelligent, beautiful women who have my head and heart spinning. I can't decide on which one to concentrate my energies. I am withdrawing from the dating race for a while. I hope you will understand."

I wished him well and wrote a final message, commending him for his straightforward behavior.

Months later, around Christmas time, he wrote a warm note asking for an update on how I was doing. I answered as a casual friend would, not indicating any need to continue communication. He is now gone forever. I hope that he has found someone to appreciate him. Perhaps he has, perhaps not. Jerry became one of the many stories without an ending that I accumulated on my way to Make It Happen.

Familiar Route

We all need some means of keeping on course when the going gets rough. Let's not forget about Hank, the fellow with the wife in a nursing home. He was my "all's right with the world" when the current acquaintances would indicate otherwise. We enjoyed dinners, concerts, and shopping. All were nonthreatening, noncommittal times, just pleasant sharing. We were fortunate to have one another at a time when he was unavailable and I was uncertain about my end goals. As noted before, everyone should have a Hank. He is still very special to me.

Lots to See on the Way

I almost forgot to mention Ricardo. Ricardo was a dentist from Brazil who had been practicing in the United States for thirty some years. He still maintained a condo and a private plane that he used when he returned to Brazil to visit his mother. It was a good thing that we were able to become acquainted through our writing. Even after all those years communicating with English, he still had a heavy accent that was difficult to decipher, almost impossible on the phone, but he was the dearest man, so polite and graciously accommodating, the ultimate gentleman. "My mother taught me well," he said. She did indeed.

Ricardo always gave me a hug in greeting but made no attempt at any deeper sexual involvement.

After a number of indulgent dinners and sublime symphony concerts, he invited me to his home. We were to have after dinner tea when he asked, "Would you like the grand tour? I just had my daughter's room papered." (His daughter worked in France.)

And that's when I saw another side of Richardo. His bedroom was elaborately furnished, accented with bright reds and guess what: the eyebrow-raising ceiling mirror above the bed. At some other time, this cool man had been hot, and perhaps he was still, but not with this girl. I remember that I was careful not to step into the room.

We remained friends for several years with the occasional call on holidays. We just weren't meant to be "one and onlys." An update email came from him just last month.

Wrong Turn

Without realizing it, we often take a wrong turn and get stuck on that road until we find an alternative way to get back on course. I'm sure that Will was a top-rated math teacher. He had the presence of a man in charge. He was tall, broad shouldered, and definitely would have been an imposing figure in front of a classroom of teenagers. He was waiting in front of the designated restaurant, and as I approached, I felt like one of those teenagers. He studied me up and down without the expected welcoming smile.

"Hello there. You must be Will. I can tell from your picture." I delivered this stupid comment tentatively.

He frowned and replied, "Yes I am, and I'm pleased that you didn't post a picture taken twenty years ago like the last woman I met."

I passed the first test, but he hadn't passed mine. I knew this was not a match but felt obligated to wait it out and proceed with lunch. Besides, I was hungry.

We were escorted to a table and handed menus, and we sat like well-trained students studying the multiple choices. We exchanged a few forced conversation starters. "I always like salads that someone else has to make." "I didn't expect this rain." "Have you been here before?" "Do you like coffee with your meal?" "Like to travel?" I wondered if his classes were this stimulating. Poor kids.

Finally, the waitress came. Will ordered first as if I, the lovely lady across from him ready to be treated like an honored guest, did not exist. Come on, ladies first. Little did he know that this action set the death knoll ringing. I made it through the meal with little conversation, already anticipating the "Dear John" email that I would send. Sometimes the written word is easier on both than the faltering, stammering spoken word left hanging there, waiting for a befuddled response.

Lessons Learned

This road was a necessary route toward my goal. It's easy to look at the array of pictures and profiles and feel that a match is just around the corner. I wanted to get on with it. Somewhere in the numbers, I had to find The Right One. The journey just described hit only the highlights of some of my defining episodes. There were many more.

This approach to dating is unlike any other because of the bounce-back opportunity. The old adage of other fish in the sea rings true, unlike the limitations in the school or community dating fields. You hit the screen again, try different sites, and take a second look at an earlier "skim over." However, if you have a series of rejections, you may need to take a look at your profile. Is it positive? Does it display an out-going personality that attracts? Is your photograph a most becoming one, smiling, welcoming? Take a serious look at the profiles that you are attracted to. Do they really reflect your list of "must haves"? Are you a "must have" in return for those particular ones? Check your "must have" list again. Are you sticking to it, or did you stray toward to an appealing smile or income?

Who decides to end a relationship that just started? It can be either person. The fairness factor is in being immediate, not furthering a hopeless association just to have a date on Saturday night or a free lunch. It is important to accept the common-sense decision to retreat before feelings grow any deeper. You can avoid that feeling of rejection or the guilt of hurting someone. There should be no regrets, only a sense of relief that a doomed relationship ended before someone got hurt. You may feel disappointed, but early recognition and acceptance of a useless relationship is paramount. If you are the one provoking the termination, it is courteous to let the other person know. Don't just drop out of sight. Rob experienced this with Julia, and I had with Charlie: the hurting, sudden termination of a relationship without explanation. It may be difficult to explain your reason for leaving, but in all fairness to that other devoted person, please take the time to gently account for your action.

You will be free to try again. Remember that you both are shopping, and "If it doesn't fit you, don't take it home." Chances are that the person's profile didn't fit your shopping list in the first place. That's why those profiles are so important. We will again tackle creating and studying profiles in a later chapter.

This may be your first dating experience in a number of years. This is the opportunity to learn more about yourself and your preferences at this time of your life. Realize that we are in a new social climate that calls for women to be much more aggressive in the dating scene. You can make the first move in contacting. You can suggest a phone call. You can ask for a coffee date. Making It Happen requires initiative, and it is now socially acceptable for women to make those first moves.

Monday morning quarterbacking allows me to analyze the anticipated relationships that never happened. Better care in the selection process would have made such a difference, but I sometimes got carried away with the adventure of it all. It was a delight to experience the newness of each candidate and to take advantage of the prolific choices offered on the Internet.

Repeated Pattern

This time it certainly looks for real!
The right location, two miles away.
We share so much in common
We want to meet without delay. *Anticipation*

One more time of disappointment
After feeling so sure that he was the one.
He was just too dull as I endured our meeting
Bored with the static, anything but fun. *Rejection*

Reading through false profiles,
Seeing pictures that are old,
Waiting for the nonresponders.
The repetition leaves me cold. *Frustration*

So is there someone out there?
Is it worth still searching more?
I must try once again to find him.
No hesitation, only feeling sure. *Determination*

When I reflect on my adventures, I wonder how those "frogs" are doing. I hope they have found the right person. I can readily see that I was not that right person. Rejection was my friend in the end.

Now let's share a real success story, when I found a priceless gem in a pile of stones. Someone who would change my life forever was just around the corner.

Chapter 6—Meeting of the Minds

My Good Knight

That shining gem was someone who would enrich each day with a creative spark so valued by a writer. Who says a muse must be female?

It began in December 2007. He was just another fellow who peeked at my profile on one of the sites. I looked at his picture and was pleased with the very appealing face. He had a warm smile and sported a devilish look in his eyes. Add a beard and he could have passed as a professor.

His profile immediately appealed to me. "I have a lot of interests. Fortunately, all these interests are portable. I can take them anywhere and get them anywhere: books, music, art, dining, dancing, travel, and walking. And I have lots of friends. Let us enjoy another's company once more. Let us laugh. Let this be the best time of our lives. There's only one problem. I have no one to share all this with, the best part of my life and hopefully hers." He went on about his free state. Good health, virtually no family obligations, businesses and properties sold.

His name was Rob, and he lived in Cleveland, inviting challenges for scalding repartee concerning the Steelers and the Browns. We discovered a mutual interest in marketing. Rob had had his own advertising agency and a sales promotion firm. Although my degrees were in music, my bread-and-butter job was in marketing for senior communities. Little did we realize then that the shared skills acquired in marketing would prompt such creative writing between us.

During Rob's time on the Internet, he had been appalled at the gross handles that other men used in their profiles. To establish his courteous manner with women, he decided that his handle should be "Good Knight." Rob became my Good Knight, and I was his Lady of the Knight Joan. (Joan is my middle name.) The Internet was our Camelot.

And here I am again, Marti's Good Knight Rob. She has asked me to join her in this chapter to share the experiences and the impressions we had of each other as our relationship progressed. While there is no right way or wrong way for people to introduce themselves in these matters, I think you will see the qualities of honesty, moving slowly, humor, openness, and compassion that formed a solid basis for a lasting relationship.

As our exchanges increased in frequency and as Christmas approached, I wrote: "And I heard him exclaim as he drove out of sight . . . Merry Christmas to all and to all a Good Knight. I've found him! The Good Knight that Santa has talked of all these years. It's YOU!! Infamous, notorious you! What a find, kinda like the Holy Grail. I may even pay for the coffee. Until then, merry, merry Christmas. Marti."

I had found my Good Knight.

Frankly, I was a little scared! "Ho, ho, ho" might turn to "Oh, oh, oh."

Caring

December was the anniversary of the death of Rob's beloved wife, JoAnn, and he admitted that some years seemed harder than others as he talked about their final days together. He was a loving caregiver who had made the final days as full of life as possible. During this time, I tried to keep my emails to him positive and upbeat. I remember sending him some of my humorous limericks and some thoughts of encouragement to help him through this time. He seemed such a special person that I wanted to ease his pain. Here are a few samples.

Melt Down

There once was a snowman named Fuddle
Who wanted to warm up and cuddle
He drank some hot tea,
Then started to pee.
And now he is simply a puddle.

Street Scene

I once had a friend named Sue
Who created quite a to-do.

In tight jeans she bent,
The back seam it went,
And guys on the street loved the view.

Lessons I have learned about grief:

For each it is an individual experience.
One step forward, two steps back is to be expected.
Be grateful for the special times you had together that some have never experienced.

Memories are treasures meant to be enjoyed with frequent recounting.

Happiness must come from within....not dependent on someone else.

I never have to stop the loving or being loved by that special someone.

Pictures are to be displayed, making a statement of that lasting love.

The grief will not dramatically disappear; it just quietly diminishes.

I wrote, "So my friend, move softly through this remembrance time in any way it might manifest itself. It's yours to experience. I will not expect to hear from you until you pass through this time. So I will say Merry Christmas in whatever way you celebrate it and hope that your New Year will be filled with satisfied wishes. Marti."

Marti's perception and sensitivity to my personal situation at this time of year spoke to my inner self, "Fear not, Good Knight, she is real and very special."

By January, we were on a roll that continued as many words were exchanged.

On January 20, 2009, I wrote, "Afternoon Rob,

Off to get a haircut and a question came to mind. Do two-headed people have to pay for two haircuts? Or are the fees based on one butt, one chair? Having crossed eyes, do I get into movies at half price because only one eye can be directed at the screen? Just curious. Marti."

Rob responded: "Personally I like the Butt Method of Validation in the barber chair. The movie theater will point out that you can turn your head at will and use the other eye. Full price. Extending that out to the two heads, they should pay double. However, the attached one butt brings it back to a single price ticket. That's marketing. Isn't it wonderful being weird? Rob."

Weirdness still works for me, Marti, especially the kind we share.

Convergence

At the end of January, it was time to plan a meeting. Sharon, Pennsylvania, was a midway point for us, with a well-known shoe store that we had visited many times on our own. We were both shoe addicts.

We met in the parking lot, and no one had to introduce us. We just knew. We exchanged a joyous hug, the first of many to come. As we hustled toward the shoe store, the spoken words started flowing. The unspoken email words were now coming alive. The relationship was at a new level.

We enjoyed perusing the store, sharing our shoe addiction. We critically assessed the beauty of these foot coverings, scowling at the uglies and praising the beauties. I did succumb to a stunning pair of black fabric flats. (They will always be a reminder of that first meeting.) We found a restaurant that was elegantly wood paneled and filled with business folks on their lunch hour. Our lunch hour extended into several hours tucked away in a corner booth. We exchanged more intimate stories about past relationships, family, and careers. It was a special time.

As we parted, Rob cleaned the snow off my car, a gesture that a man had not done for me in many years. I handed him a tin of homemade ginger cookies to sustain him on his drive home. (The tin of cookies became a much repeated gesture on my part.) This was one of the few times I wanted to see someone again. Bravo, Rob!

I never told Marti that I was seriously planning to wear a suit of armor to that first meeting, but I couldn't imagine driving nearly 100 miles in a suit of armor—let alone what the turnpike toll attendant would say or do. And despite our emails, upon first sight she might say to herself, "This is too weird" and burn rubber out of Sharon without even going into the world's largest shoe store. I knew that day Marti was a little suspicious that I didn't buy any shoes. I was losing credibility because in earlier emails I mentioned my passion for penny loafers, etc. What she didn't know was that I had been informed of a shoe inheritance heading my way.

Compassion for Shoes

A later email verified the shoe fetish.

"Greetings My Fair Lady. I'm still at home suffering from the worst cold of the century. Pass the Vicks. A friend in my old condo called me and said, 'What size shoe do you wear?' Turns out my friend is the executor for a wealthy doctor's estate, and the doc loved shoes! (No, not Dr. Scholl's. Be serious, Marti) The late doctor's foot is the same size as mine!

I now have twenty-nine additional pairs of shoes to add to my collection!!! Spectators, lizard skin slip-ons, golf cleated bucks, even a pair of Mephistos. Talk about one foot in the grave! Some are approximate duplicates of my own collection, which I will sort and pass on to some deserving locker-room buddy and foot fiend. Even then, I'll have about forty pairs. I'm already trying to reconfigure my closet and get added shoe racks. In my one-bedroom, that ain't going to be easy."

"Knowing our mutual fetish, I hope you will take this in a positive manner and wish me Happy Insteps or Lots of Soles and no Heels. I know we are both too proper to let our shoe's tongue protrude provocatively. Emelda.

P.S. During my illness, I had the new additions all lined up in my living room as I unpacked them. Me thinks the good doctor isn't letting go too easily. I swear the next morning they were lined up differently, this for several nights in a row. Do you have the phone number for Ghostbusters?"

"Dear Emelda,

I'm afraid you have tapped into a world unknown to the straight and narrow. The day we were at the shoe store you deceived the gods by ignoring your impulses and shunning a new pair. We are born to certain fetishes, and it is wrong to deny those endowed rights. I will not go so far as to suggest that you were responsible for the doc's death, but it might have pushed the due date a little. And you notice you were knocked silly with a cold by the gods to enhance your helplessness. This is more than circumstance. Of all the deserving shoeless people in the world, why were you The Chosen? And why twenty-nine pairs? What does that signify? Think of the events in the your twenty-ninth year, particularly the shoes you wore—a little tight fitting, worn down at the heels, a little out of style? Or what was happening when your original shoe collection was at twenty-nine pairs? Numerology demands some connection here. And yes, these shoes were meant for walking, so they did move around to adjust to their new home. Beware when you will 'bewareing' them. Beware of 'ware' they take you. If someone addresses you as Doc, get to Barefoot status ASAP."

Purification of hand-me-down shoes: invite three friends over as witnesses. Put each pair of shoes on the opposite foot, no socks. Cross the right foot over the left, right hand on left ear lobe with left hand on right buttock. Step back three steps, reciting 'Shoe be mine' with each step. Reverse hands and feet, and move forward four steps, not three, as you recite 'Shoe be do' with each step.

Your partner in 'feetish,' Marti.

P.S. If we stuff the toes a little, could I borrow the lizard slip-ons?"

Rob responded:

"You win, Marti. This is extremely clever and funny. I may still be a little under the weather, but even if I were at the top of my game, I cannot approach your verve and wit. Is that why I'm known as the village HALF-wit?

Only one thing you missed, the masculine of Emelda. In the interim, I roll over to Emelda Man.

Good Knight Rob.

P.S. Perhaps I'll redo my coat of arms with a montage of shoes and a motto of Stubbed Toe???"

China Bound

There were times that we communicated by snail mail. I opened my mail box on July 10, 2008 and was surprised to see a business envelope from Rob. I was saddened by what I read.

"This is farewell, Marti, for I'm off to Japan and an entirely new career, one that I feel entirely suited for in both age and vigor. One in which my hearing problem will not be a deterrent.

The enclosed article explains all.

Wish me well. And when I reach star status, I'll send you autographed photos. Lucky you??? Then, at soirées and family reunions, you can drop little hints that you 'knew him when' etc.

So it's goodbye Good Knight, hello Round-Eyed Samurai!

Stay in touch. Yours in nothing at all [then came a series of Japanese hieroglyphics], Rob-san."

By now, I knew this was just the thing to get Marti's writing all afrothing. I could hardly contain myself in expectation.

The enclosed article from *Time*, July 7, 2008 was headlined "Postcard: Tokyo."

It began, "As sex lives sag, an aging society is seeing a boom in pornography appealing to—and starring—Japan's septuagenarian set. Where older dogs are learning new tricks."

My sadness lifted to a level of extreme curiosity. It seemed that Shigeo Tokuda (a stage name), a seventy-three-year-old man, has cashed in on the adult film industry's demand for "elder porn." Japan had been found to be one of the most sexless societies in the industrialized world. Tokuda shared a lifetime of expertise in films that were watched by old and young alike. Japan's largest video stores introduced about a thousand films each month, and about three hundred of these featured mature women.

My curiosity soared to overwhelming humor as I pictured Rob in his new fantasized role. It demanded an immediate email response.

"Dear Rob-san,

It breaks my heart to write this email to you. I am so ashamed and feeling so guilty. I am truly devastated.

When I accepted my new job, I never thought giving your name and my preacher's name as references would lead to such a result. The preacher gave his notice last week, simply explaining that he would be accepting a position doing missionary work in Japan (or was it missionary position?).

When you arrive to do your *thing*, if you are coupled with a voluptuous, sexy female wearing a bag over her head, just proceed for Old Glory and your own delight. Please don't speak my name.

I hope you can forgive me for redirecting your life. May all your jobs be exciting and satisfying.

Stay in touch. Yours with a bag, Marti-san."

Rob emailed back:

"Dear Marti-san,

Of course I forgive you. Your referral has (pardon the expression) opened up an entire new view of life and relationships.

It has made me young again, although I did temporarily feel a little older and rather exhausted after my last take when she blurted her lines, 'Take me, I'm yours', for the fifteenth take.

And be not shy about your new career. Be proud. Remove that sack or you might get sacked, or most certainly hyperventilate. (Is that perhaps how you get yourself into character?)

Last night I had a dream. I was starring in a flick called "Harem Scarum." (Apologies to the Marx Bros.) I enter the harem dressed as Kid Caliph. There are sixty-nine harem ladies, each with a sack over their head. As I "enter-tain" each, one by one, I whisper into their sack, 'Is that you, Marti?' Oh, the reactions I get.

Right now I'm starring in a film entitled "Puppy Love." No missionary work. More puppy stuff. See you around the set.

Is this staying in touch? Or is that another kind of touching?

Yours with a smile [Japanese hieroglyphics], Rob-san.

P.S. I see your preacher is starring in a film entitled "Peaches and the Preacher." I hear it's a Cecil B. DeMille spectacular. Opening scene: Sermon on the Mount (beats me how you can talk at a time like that). Can hardly wait for the scene, Parting of the . . ."

Still laughing, I responded:

"UNCLE!!! You win. That was the best of the best. I must leave it on that high note! Sat at my computer reading and laughing out loud, hating for it to end. Lady with the Bag."

What can I say? How could a Good Knight become an aging Japanese porno star? Only in fantasy. As long as it stays there, it is quite a lot of fun. I now sign emails to Marti as "GK-san" (GK for Good Knight, "san" as a reminder of my supposed film prowess).

Competing

As part of the ongoing banter of Browns versus Steelers, one other snail mail letter reported Rob's concern that Cleveland Home Security had discovered he was communicating with a *Stealer* fan: "There's a group of irate people gathering beneath my balcony with torches and tar." The bottom corner of the stationery had been burned away!

Coastal Trip

When Rob left for a visit with his son on the East Coast, he promised to have the pilot do a flyover so that he could wave to me. The appointed day of the earth-to-sky communication came and went.

When he was home again, I wrote:

"The next time we plan a flyover, we need to make a major change. Instead of waving, I'm simply going to hold up a 'Hi Rob, Marti Says Hello' sign. As I waved, the man three seats behind you got all excited and was waving back in absolute delight. I was so embarrassed!"

Rob replied,

"That's was only part of the story. He wouldn't calm down. You must be really something when you wave. On the descent into Newark, he was still so excited that he took off a shoe, waved it frantically, and we all hit the deck. One fearless steward leaped up and subdued him. The demented man was carried off in a straight-jacket, mumbling passionately, 'Marti, Marti, Marti.' A get-well card from you might help. Send it to Bellevue.

Oddly enough, I too have had these uncontrollable urges around you. Do you do this to all men? Or just to knights living in the past or an occasional frequent flyer? GK-san."

Cherishing

Was it all fun and games? No, we had our serious, caring sides. You already heard about the sharing of grief concerns. His granddaughter's diagnosis of diabetes at age seven, or my major quandary about whether to rebuild the transmission in a ten-year-old car or purchase a new one. When Rob had a tedious day with water damage to his apartment, I knew that I should not console him with the written word. I called him to commiserate. The next day he wrote, "What seemed to be shaping up as a blowout day (yesterday) turned out to be wonderful because of hearing your voice and feeling the caring. Thank thee, thank thee. This Knight slept well last night because of you."

There's a time to be weird and funny and a time to be compassionate. Marti seems to get it right every time. Thank you.

Rob and I spent over two years with intensive communication and periodic fun visits. We were able to experience each other at some unseen, but definitely soul felt level. Prior to one of his summer visits I received this: "Shh. Listen. It's the whinny of an excited steed. The slow clip-clop of hooves, then faster and faster, now trotting, now racing the wind. The slap of a sword in its scabbard. The angle of chain mail and armor. The ca-ching of turnpike toll booths a'tolling. The clarion cry of a Knight of all Knights, 'Hi Ho Pittsburgh.' And away we are to see our Fair Lady Joan. There's a lot at stake."

Hopefully, not you at the stake, Joan. Every several months, there was a get together, from a spectacular Chihuly glass exhibit at the Phipp's Conservatory or a tour of Henry Clay Frick's home with lunch at the Cafe. Or just a nice dinner at a unique area restaurant. Nothing special and yet so very special.

Crunchy Cookies

After another tin of cookies was sent for no reason but to spoil him, Rob wrote:

"Munch, munch, munch.

Munch, munch? Munch, munch, munch, munch. Munch, munch, munch, munch, munch.

Munch, munch, munch.

GK munch, munch, san"

Lessons Learned

What absolute delight I felt to have discovered such a special person! He was a far cry from many I had experienced. As satisfied with this find as I felt, was I writing to and seeing other men during this time? Certainly. I was on a "Make It Happen" mission. You don't stop shopping just because a delightful distraction turns your head, but no one was going to take Rob out of my shopping cart.

This is one Good Knight that wants to remain in the shopping cart. It is more than the cookies.

Chapter 7—Your Journey Begins

Whatta Site

Ready to head out on *your* exciting journey? Ready to "Make It Happen" for you? Let's review the steps. Choosing a site is not as binding as choosing a mate. If you don't like your original selection, you can easily move to another. There are many choices. There is no magic formula for selection. If one site looks particularly appealing to you, just jump in and see if the temperature is right.

Your first step will be to go on a search of senior sites. Simply Google 'Senior dating site reviews' and the search results will list sites with descriptions, number of members, and reviews. There you can benefit by the experieces of others.

You'll find that the sites vary in cost. Plenty of Fish. com is a national service that is completely free, and it may be a good place to start until you feel comfortable about the whole scene. Be aware that many sites renew your active status automatically when they have your credit card number. You must notify them if you want to drop the service.

As you check out a site, you will be encouraged to join. Some places entice you by offering a free search. After showing the picture and opening lines of several attractive profiles, a questionnaire appears, encouraging you to join if you want to see the complete profiles or if you want to see the rest of the candidates that match your preference.

Should you list on more than one site? Cost is the first consideration. Over the period of six months or a year, the amount can be considerable. I always thought of it as part of my entertainment money. Believe me, it was entertainment. If you decide to use more than one site, it might be wise to use a different picture and/or to change the emphasis of your profile. I ran into many other people who were on various sites, some repeating the same information and others who were quite creative with different approaches. For instance, if you mention fishing as one of your active interests, this can be expressed in different ways: "I enjoy the back-to-nature feel of being on the water on a quiet lake" or "Nothing is as exciting as the bob of the fishing line as the captive trout plunges to his doom." How about this? "My favorite place for retreating from the world is at the end of a fishing pole." You get the picture.

One time I purposely responded to the same person on two sites. I became the person they were seeking in each profile. The man responded to both, wanting to know more. We both enjoyed the humor when I admitted my double identity. I only did this once, because it could irritate some people.

When you subscribe to a site, you will be asked a set of questions. Great care should be taken with your answers in fairness to yourself and others. The questionnaires may inquire about your preferences in religion, education, income, occupation, and number of children. Some ask you to check off your preferences on a long list. If you are not comfortable with certain religions or with a lack of faith, that is the time to express it. If you are an intellectual with many degrees, you may feel a need to limit responders to those of a similar background. You're not going for quantity of respondents but for high-quality, screened ones suited specifically to your "must haves." When you specify your interests, stop and think about what is really of interest to you. These need to be activities that you have experienced and want to continue doing. Do not check skydiving if you've never done it—this is not a "can you top this" list. What you check off should well define who you are and who you are seeking.

The eHarmony site requires extensive psychological testing, claiming to find your perfect match. My experience with the site was very negative. I think it selects all candidates whether or not they are active. It was like pulling teeth to get any response from these "perfect" matches. Not worth my money. On the other sites, you can make your own choices and can see how active the members are. You can see the last time a member logged on to the site, and if it is more than three months ago, I wouldn't bother contacting. You want someone online "now" or someone who has been online in the last couple weeks. Those are the active pursuers who are still alive and breathing.

If you are over sixty years old, keep in mind that this mature age group is just now building its computer savvy. There were few of us a couple years ago, but now we are one of the fastest growing groups using computers. It has taken us a while to learn the system and to trust it. As the numbers grow, the availability of potential dating candidates grows.

If you have investigated private dating services, you will immediately see a much lower cost online. I don't feel the private services are an advantage for seniors. So few seniors invest in them that you will be matched with anyone close to your age, not a carefully selected person. This is true despite all the personality matching tests given up front. Save that choice for those young critters. I knew one man who filled in when an older man was needed even though his membership had long since expired. I also appreciate making my own choices rather than being subjected to someone else's poor choices for me!

Who Am I?

Your next challenge is writing a profile. If I had to do it all over again, I might start with my profile even before selecting a site. That way I would have my "resume" in hand before applying, and it might have helped in site selection. I would have been sure of "who" was looking for "what" if I had to work on defining myself first. Your profile is your smile, your handshake, your confident manner, your best foot forward, your first impression all wrapped up in words. Somewhere early in childhood, many of us were taught not to promote ourselves with boastful statements. It is acceptable to make honest statements about ourselves in today's society, but for some of us, it is still difficult to "blow our own horn." Many of the profiles I have read start out with apologies about sounding boastful. Get over it. Words are your only sales tools in this highly competitive game. In your profile, you have a limited amount of space to give all the reasons that you are unique and desirable, plus a little about the person who would attract this special you. I found that a number of people used "My friends say that I . . ." as an easy way to list complimentary remarks about themselves.

Let's start with a list of the facts, not the "I wish I were" dreams. You have to back up your statements with truths that will hold up upon meeting. If you list yourself as a nonsmoker, that means you *are* a nonsmoker, not a smoker trying to quit. List the words people use when they compliment you: funny, loyal, honest, fashionable, good cook, leader, etc. Combine a couple in a sentence: "I'm known as a preferred leader probably due to the fact that I can have fun with those I am leading, sometimes a little sarcasm, sometimes just plain old corny" or how about, "I'm an enthusiastic cook, but a reluctant bottle washer." If you're a traveler, mention the states or countries that you have visited. If you have lived in several different cities, list them. This creates an open door for comments from someone contacting you and is a step beyond just responding to interests and activities.

You may find it extremely helpful to read other profiles, but I would do one on yourself first. You want this to be your own. It's *you* in the spotlight. What makes you unique?

Anyone can write "I love to walk." Instead try, "I love to walk in the coolness of evening in a park near the river." Paint a picture. Anyone can write, "Love dining out." Instead try, "I love to eat in an ethnic restaurant and pretend I'm really in that country." Again, draw a picture. Instead of "Have three grandkids," wouldn't you rather read, "I have a triangle of grandkids: Minneapolis, Atlanta, and Phoenix"? This makes the reader much more interested in responding. Illustrate your uniqueness.

I wish I had known all this when I originally wrote my profile. I revised it as I traveled along and got a little smarter.

Avoid describing your complete history. You want to stay in the now with a touch of the future. Retelling your history is great for coffee time or over lunch, and remember that history must be of your individual experiences, not other relationships.

As I read profiles, the greatest turnoff for me was the line "I'll tell you later."

There was no "later" for these fellows as far as I was concerned. If you can't know more about a person from their personal history, how can you know if they are a real candidate for your future? Some even state, "Tell you later, send a message." A message about what and to whom? This was particularly true of male profiles. Do they really want women who are so desperate that they would encourage a completely unknown person? Don't give in to this, ladies. I made the mistake just once when I read the compelling interest list of a candidate who lived just five miles from me. Where his profile should have been, there was a note that said "This member has not yet submitted a profile." After the most boring lunch in the history of mankind, I could have written the illuminating profile about him. Lesson learned.

There's nothing wrong with asking a friend to critique your profile, and while they are at it, have them check your spelling. Spell checking is not included on most sites. One fellow wrote, "I always strive for *excellance*." I don't think he was being humorous by misspelling excellence. The rest of the writing was quite serious, as you would expect from someone seeking excellence, he just didn't check his spelling. Another fellow was insistent about the need for good *comunnication*. If it is that important, it deserves a spell check.

Don't write as one man did, "I am looking for that special woman who will walk with me, not in front of or behind me, but hand in hand through the rest of our loving lives together. Must live within five miles." Sorry, honey, if she were the girl next door, you would have found her by now!

Here's a better one: "I am looking for a woman that would be as faithful and supportive of me as I would be of her. I want to share all with her and be there when she needs me. As far as the style of relationship, it could be marriage or life partners. You decide." It was nice and concise.

What are your goals? Are you looking for a pen pal, marriage, or dating? It may matter considerably to the person reading the profile. Have you really thought that through? These are real people and deserve direct honesty from you. I have heard repeated complaints from online friends about dishonesty: not really single, one hundred pounds over claimed weight, older than pictured, not sure of what they want in a relationship, not really skilled in activities listed. The truth will come out, so put it out there to start. There is someone out there looking for you: "There's a lid for every pot." Remember that list of "must haves." and don't settle for less.

Say Cheese

Let's go to pictures. You will receive much more attention when you post a picture. Some people post up to ten pictures, showing various aspects of their lives. Occasionally there's a cute picture of two-year-old "Jimmy on the Pony," but what does that do for him now? The ideal pictures are taken in the past two years.

Your picture needs to support the total picture you have portrayed through your profile, including your list of interests and activities. One gentleman chose the user name "Grampsfun," which sounded appealing, but in his picture, he had his head on his hand, his lips bent down, and his eyes half closed. There was no further information. It certainly didn't look like a Gramps who was fun.

If you talk in your profile about being a great golfer, how about a picture of your golf swing? For a fisherman, the latest string of fish.

Dressing appropriately is often ignored. I am not interested in a picture of a fellow with his hairy chest staring at me. A torn t-shirt doesn't make it or a fellow wearing a hat in the house to hide a bald head that will shine upon meeting him.

Be extremely cautious about the background of the picture. That unmade bed or dirty dishes in the sink are real turnoffs.

Some pictures show grandchildren (not a favored exploitation of those dear little ones). In a group picture, others in the picture may be far more attractive! It may be a great picture of you, but if your past mate is there with you, it's a real turnoff! I have seen some photos where the past mate is cropped out but the man's arm is extended where it had been around her shoulder.

One picture showed an extremely obese gentleman. At that weight, he was a walking heart attack. He had lost the weight and wanted to doubly impress someone when they met him in person, but he couldn't understand why more women didn't want to meet him for coffee.

I have seen many pictures of poor souls who held the camera in front of themselves, and they will go down in history as "distorted frozen fish face." I have seen pictures of men still wearing their wedding band. Turnoff!

Remember that you are the product you are selling. You must portray yourself as attractively as possible.

Your photo is an important selling tool in the dating race. You want it to support the "picture" you gave in your profile. If your profile indicates that humor is an important part of your routine, don't use a picture where you are frowning.

If necessary, call a friend to take the photo for you. It will be worth it.

If you think, "But I don't know how to submit a picture," the site will provide you with step-by-step help for posting one (or ask any grandchild for help!). It is to your advantage to change your picture after six months. You don't want to broadcast the fact that you're still looking. Change the look, post one at a time, and save the others for later.

Searching

Let's charge ahead on a search! Throw caution to the wind and just scan the smorgasbord of candidates. See some samples of what's out there!

Here's a fellow looking for a younger woman. Is he up front about it? You betcha. His user name is 50PLUSWOMEN. He's forty-eight, good looking, high income, never married. He describes in detail the older woman he is seeking. He adds at the end that "if your needs, wants, and desires in life do not include the love, respect and attention of someone quite a few years younger than yourself, do NOT waste my time and yours." Right up front. Like him or not, you have to respect his forthrightness. He goes on to say that he wishes there were a separate site for those who are interested in an intergenerational relationship. Maybe he should start one. There are quite a few out there looking for just that.

Here's one: "Optimistic personality. Retired. Worked as a construction manager. Actively engaged in wood working. Own my home. Like traveling, dining, theater, movies, gardening, sports. Civil engineering degree. Looking for loving companion, with a zest to live and seek new horizons for the rest of our lives." Want to meet Joe? I did. He was exactly as he claimed. He remains a friend today. And that "loving companion"? I am happy to report that he has found her!

Many folks give away clues about their lifestyle and personality. "You get so lonesome at times when you live by yourself." Look for other depressive signs with this person. Would he settle for anyone just to have someone? "I don't have a car. The kids took it away after the accident." What caused the accident? Physical problems? Is he just looking for a driver? "Don't get out much." Why? Don't get caught up with feeling sorry for them. Once into a relationship, you may feel even sorrier for yourself! Here's one that wants a woman who is "bright, but not too talkative." That's a highly defined requirement and may be tough to find.

I find humor a real attraction as I roam the sites. Here's a fellow that says he has "blue-collar brawn with white collar brains." He is "a toucher and expects a hug instead of a handshake when we meet." He wants his woman to be "kitchen capable, not captive" and says, "I have never been known to lose my car in a parking lot." (Clever way to dispel concerns about dementia.) He finishes with, "Remember: Life is short, Break the rules, Forgive quickly. Kiss slowly. Love truly. Laugh uncontrollably, and never regret anything that makes you smile." He appears to be quite an appealing, outgoing person.

Here are some highlights from an engineer who says, "Forget the jokes about engineers, my left and right brain work together. I love to cook and can't pass up cleaning a dirty fridge. I have a soft spot for animals, always fighting the urge to take home that stray." He's warm and light-hearted.

How about this one? "Seeking a woman who believes that 'roughing it' means a hotel with no room service after midnight." Using humor gives a sense of familiarity and openness—there is a real human being behind the words.

Many of the sites give ample room to describe what you are looking for in a mate. Here's a seventy-year-old man who spells it out quite succinctly. "I aim to meet a professional lady, in her mid-sixties and up, active, and in good health. Ideally a widow still retaining her interest in the well-being of her family and friends. A good companion who keeps well informed on national and world affairs in order to maintain intelligent conversation. Would like to travel within and outside the U.S., also hike in the woods, hills, and along waterfronts, and take regular outdoor walks as one of the means of maintaining good health. A nonsmoker and without any previous serious illnesses that occasionally emerge from remission. Knows that trust in and respect for each other are essential ingredients to a good companionship. Kind, honest, considerate and sincere. Interested in serious, long-term relationship." Whew! You know as you read this that you should not take liberties with the requirements. There's nothing wrong with his being specific. You either fit the bill or you don't. You can only hope that he will not be deluged with unqualified women.

I was always a little hesitant to get involved with someone if children wrote and submitted their silent parent to the dating game. This is not a third-party game. I was also leery about ones that were sexist in their remarks. Phrases like "all women" or "just like a man" signify some clouded attitudes.

One revealed a "do it my way" attitude, saying, "I'm living within the safety of a lifestyle carefully altered to suit my personality needs." No interest in disturbing this one!

Ready for the tacky ones? Back in chapter 2, my dear coauthor shook a finger at fellows who were too suggestive too soon. Remember you haven't even met this person yet! Here are some of the direct ones that have little appeal for a woman who is looking for a long-term relationship.

Under a heading that asks what they are looking for in a partner, I found these descriptions:

- "I am looking for a very sexual relationship. A woman that that enjoys sex and will put effort into making sex better." That's all he wants.
- "As a widower, I guess the most accurate way to describe what I am looking for is a friend with benefits." We're not talking hospitalization and retirement here!
- "I'm easy going, open minded, like a lot of outdoor activities and adult fun—kissing, touching, mutual oral, toys, oil, trying new things. Also phone, cyber, in person. Like outdoor activities and a lot of adult fun and being played with." It sounds to me like indoor activities are much more a necessity for him than the outdoor ones!

Some use the direct approach in their user name: clitlover, 69best, Stillable, cum4u. If he uses "Companionhot," does that mean casual sex? I do not wish to play a guessing game. I am not being judgmental here. If that's the only reason a man wants a woman, at least he is being up front about it, but most of the women I know who are going this route are not looking primarily for sex. The sites that promote these types of liaisons would be a better place for these men to post an ad. Sexual prowess in capturing a mature woman has minimal importance. Too bad that some guys have yet to understand this.

Refinement

Instead of this nonspecific approach, let's look carefully at the real prospects. A reasonable start would be distance. It's a romantic tale when two people can relate that despite being on separate coasts, they fell in love through the Internet, but it's not too practical or common. There may have been other circumstances such as family or mutual friends living in that distant area. You will be much more successful staying closer to home. You have an opportunity to explore particular members within a radius of twenty-five, fifty or one hundred miles. Start with twenty-five miles. You can also select age, religion, language, and other qualifications (depending on the site). You want to be as specific as possible. Give a reasonable age range. If more than one religion is acceptable to you, say so. The site will show the profiles that match. If there are none that fit your criteria, you may adjust some of the requirements, but don't make too many concessions. It is better to move to a different site. Remember that a carefully chosen person is out there for you.

I looked at profiles with or without pictures. There are some well-known people (at least in their neighborhoods) that would rather not go public with their Internet dating. Give them an opportunity to prove their worth through the written word. On the other hand, a picture may not portray your dream mate. Read the profile. They might be exactly what you're seeking. Give them a chance.

This is where the "I'll tell you later" people lose out. This is a highly competitive scene, and you need all the promotion you can get. I do forgive anyone who prefers to withhold income level—some items are better kept for later—but the initial selection of a candidate requires at least knowing his interests and what he is looking for in a mate.

When you find a likely person, you will know it. Your heart will beat a little faster as you think, "This is it! This is the one!" What next? Check on how recently they visited the site, and make sure it's within a couple weeks. You then have two choices. You can send a flirt or an email. Remember that you will be anonymous as far as your true identity and address are concerned, and you are not risking your safety at this point.

Some members specify that they do not accept flirts. That's the easy way out for the sender. No clever, original writing is involved, but when you're brand new at this game, it seems an easier way to see if you will get a response. Most sites give a list of statements, and you can select one to send. "Like your picture" or "We seem to have a lot in common" or "How about coffee?" Select one and hit "Send."

You will be far better received if you take the effort to write a few words along with a flirt. You might be tempted to tell more about yourself, but a more gracious approach is to highlight some facts about the person. "I see that you enjoy golfing. Ever play in the snow? I've seen it on local courses and wonder how they can hold a club with freezing hands." If movies are his interest, write, "What type of movies appeal to you? Interesting that so many 3D films are now available." This gives the receiver a direct way to respond. You have given him a topic and eased him into a written conversation. Chances are that he will ask specific questions about you in return.

Lessons Learned

Selecting a site for Internet dating and establishing yourself as a player is exciting. It is a move that can change the plot of your biography. You are setting forth on an adventure that could truly be life changing. Do not take it lightly. Move through this beginning stage with absolute confidence that you are the promoter of a truthful portrayal of your current self. Your honesty today can ensure a future of shared pleasure.

I am saddened by the number of times I've heard people say that they tried the Internet for dating but were not successful. They found someone they liked, wrote, talked, went on a date, and it wasn't magic. End of story.

That's only the beginning. You must be willing to go back to the screen over and over again. This pursuit is not for the weak willed, as it is a tough journey of ups and downs. Do it and do it again. Don't be put off by the wrong person. Keep looking for that right one. This can take several years, but in the meantime, you will enjoy meeting many respondents. Even if they do not end up as your life partner, they can easily become a lifelong friend. With each encounter, you will learn more about yourself and what your needs are. You'll enjoy some good coffee dates or lunches in the meantime. At least you're not sitting at home alone!

Where do you go from here? How long will it take? Stick with me. Your journey has just begun.

Chapter 8—On Your Own

Create Your Map

We have reviewed many suggestions and covered many scenarios, and now it gets highly individual. As you move along on this journey, there is no automatic pilot to help you navigate this maze of Internet dating. There is no universal map. The journey will be yours alone, with a destination of leaving the "alone" behind and moving on to togetherness. There are, however, some broad guidelines that are important.

Let's say you are enrolled in three sites. You are caught up in the joy of pursuit, feeling a little anxious in a positive way. You are ready to believe that you will hit it lucky and find that special someone right away, or within a week, but the voice of experience says, "Highly unlikely."

The stories that you hear of others finding the right person are generally the outcome of an unde-termined amount of time spent dating. Please don't give up because the first two dates were unsuccessful. Persistence is the key.

Plan a time of day to spend on exploring your sites. Your chosen sites will notify you when you have a flirt or a message. If it is a reply of any sort, consider yourself fortunate. If it is initiated by the other person, you are truly fortunate.

If you have sent someone a message, you may be anxiously awaiting a response, but unfortunately, many times the communication is never acknowledged. If this is the case, it may be better to be silent yourself.

Handle a flirt or a message in the same way: courteously. A flirt is an easy way to test the water, but it still required some action on the part of the sender. Your profile has been read and judged as acceptable. If you do not want to encourage correspondence, don't let anonymity rob you of courtesy. Send a simple note explaining that you are looking for someone closer to home (or closer to your own age or with more common interests).

If you do want to respond to a message, take a little time to think through the amount of information necessary. It's not the time to go overboard with your family history, work career, and remaining goals in life. Pull out something from the message, make comments, and then add some fresh chatty remarks about yourself, perhaps some items not included in your profile. It is not the time to give your phone number or address; you must guard that information.

There will be times when no one on the site interests you. Be patient. Keep checking each day for new arrivals. Don't be tempted to go beyond your distance range or to compromise your "must haves."

Will you have trouble keeping correspondents staight when you write to several in one day? You will find they are so individual that there will be no problem. You get to know each one as you move along. I'm sure you tried on more than one pair of shoes the last time you were shopping, and there was no confusion in telling them apart!

Say that you have been corresponding with some-one for a week or two, and suddenly there is a raging red light that says "Stop! This is not the one." Again, be courteous. You have encouraged this person, and now, because he didn't really stop smoking or has an STD, you needn't be rude. Thank him for his interest, but let him know that you are not comfortable with proceed-ing. Wish him the best in finding the right person. No harm done.

How long do you wait for a response from a new selection? If this person has been on the site within several weeks, wait two weeks. He could simply be out of town visiting the grandchildren, or perhaps he has found someone and just hasn't removed himself from the site. You do not have to go through a delete function. Only if he responds do you need an acknowledgement.

If you really want to pursue a special candidate, there is no harm in writing a second time. "I hope my first email didn't get displaced into your pile of scam mail. I would really like to hear from you." You can sim-ply repeat the words from the first contact, adding a few simple brilliant changes. Chances are the person won't even recognize it as a repeat. It is worth a try.

Let's zero in on a specific subject. Say that you have been writing for two weeks, almost every day. He really looks like a special guy, and you want to meet him. Writing does not give the satisfaction of eye contact, the warmth of a smile, voice inflection, or the charm of laughter. After a while, the electronic smiley faces lose their charm. If you ask to talk with him, will he give you his phone number? Leave nothing to chance. You may want to give him your number first (your cell phone number so that your address cannot be traced). Even if he gives no indication of being a stalker, it's always best to be on the safe side. Chances are he will either respond with his number or dial yours.

Here You Go

Let several sessions of conversation go by before asking for or accepting a specific date such as a coffee date followed by a walk, or perhaps lunch in a local restaurant. Whatever feels right. The ideal place will be quiet and relaxed. There's no harm in meeting for coffee in the morning and then being available for lunch if you find you are enjoying each other's company. These meetings can be a little scary. Share what you will be wearing so that you are easy to spot—there's nothing worse than fearing you will approach the wrong stranger! Be sure to decide on the exact meeting place ("in front of the restaurant" or "just inside the door"). You want to feel confident about your arrival.

On this first date, it's important that the woman drives herself there. This gives both of you a means of escape if the rendezvous turns sour.

You can let your best friend know where and when this meeting will take place.

The first impression looms ahead as you approach the designated meeting place. Remember to smile as you approach. Do you touch upon meeting? A handshake is certainly acceptable, but on occasion I have encouraged and welcomed a hug. It depends on how close you have become in your writing and phone conversations.

Talk about how scary this is for you. Ask questions, and tell your favorite stories about growing up. Talk about the time you put a thumbtack on the teacher's chair.

You can open up with warm tales of family, but avoid recounting past relationships. This indicates "baggage" and there's many a profile that stipulates "no baggage". Watch your use of collective pronouns. Whether you are widowed or divorced, you are no longer a *we* or *ours*. Using those terms shuts the other person out. Stick with *I, me* and *mine*. It's a strong pronouncement that you are ready to become part of a new relationship. (Rob made a point of this in chapter 4.)

Who pays the bill? Was "going Dutch" mentioned on the phone? If not, as the waitperson is taking the order, the woman should ask for a separate check, which can be argued or not by the gentleman. Even in this day and age, this seems to be the proper tactic. And fellows, if you have to pay for lunch, isn't it worth it to check out this possible relationship?

You'll sense when the first meeting should end. If you have had a pleasant time, feel free to say so. Hiding feelings can mean no follow-up call or date. It's reasonable to mention an activity that you would like to share and say, "Let me know when you're free."

If the date has been nothing more than a difficult and obligatory passage of time, you still want to be courteous and say thank you. In most cases, the negative vibes will be felt by both parties, and you will both be relieved that it's over. If an email follows the next day, it is up to you to decide how to handle the rejection. Courtesy still matters. Tell him that you feel he has much to offer to the right person and that you wish him well. Not answering at all is rude and a little heartless. I recently heard from a happy friend who is now coupled with someone she met through one of her Internet "rejects."

If all went well at the meeting and you follow up with another event, you are now getting to know the person on a more personal level. This may be The One. Give it a chance. Give it a while.

You have put time and effort into finding this person. You both may feel a chemistry that has promise, but take time to get to know each other's habits, good and bad. Experience the types of events and activities that form a solid base for a lasting relationship. Settle for caressing and cuddling—hold back on sexual intimacy until you both agree that you are ready.

Not all contacts are fruitful, but with each new contact, you have an opportunity for a connection. Each time you send a flirt or a message to a prospect, you are putting yourself out there for a possible acceptance or rejection. As you wait for a response, it is perfectly natural to fantasize about the person and his rightness for you. If you are rejected, deal with it. Perhaps the choice was not a good one anyway and you let yourself stray from your basic requirements. If necessary, you can play "justification head games." "He really wasn't what I wanted." "Never did like blue-eyed men.""Boy, is he missing out.""He'll never know how great I would be for him."

Go have a piece of dark chocolate or a bag of popcorn soaked in butter. Take a walk. Pitch in and try again. The right one is still out there!

Stop, Look, and Listen!

Guarding your personal information has already been covered, but it is so important that it must be mentioned again. Dating sites are set up to keep you anonymous. You are in control of any personal information. (There are only a few sites that do criminal checks; rumor has it that more will do this in the future.) Scam artists can be slick in both their writing and conversation. Never call the candidate using your land line; use your cell phone. Do not have him pick you up for that first meeting; you must guard your address. Always meet in a public place, and when you arrive, if you find you are the least bit suspicious of the person's intent, get out of there! Do not respond to any request to tap your assets, or you may end up as a headline.

After some time on the sites, you will be able to spot scams. There is a market out there for your email address, and you will need to protect it. A typical scammer message goes like this (spelling and punctuation as written, email address altered):

"How are you doing? I saw your profile am highly intrested in you and I will like to pick you up from there. Am a man with goood manners and sense of humor man always caring for someone who is ready to make love grow with me and care for one another. Am I a looking for woman who is responsible, passionate, caring, trustworthy woman that will make me happy all my life that will take away my sorrow that will always be there fromdoing good time And I think you are the woman that my heart desire so you can meet me on my yahoo messenger so that we can chat there this is my id (rrrrr64) this is my email address below (rrrrr64@xxxxx.com) so I will be expecting you.

Your profile is more to say about. Yours in Love, NOTE: I will like you to email me back to my personal email (rrrrr@xxxxx.com) same as my xxxxx IM. Would love to get to know u a lot. Also I would be willing to relocate for the right woman after getting to know each other better."

The misuse of the language and the insistence on personal email are immediate clues that this email is a scam. Not only do we have scammers seeking personal email addresses, but there are men in foreign countries who would like to move to America and are looking for a vulnerable woman who will bring them here.

I saw two suspicious messages, one from Texas and one from California, with different names and different personal email addresses. Both mentioned "in search of my Soul and Dream Mate" (same words, same capitalization). Both listed their activities as swimming, camping, fishing, reading, and tennis. The same activities in the same order. Both ended with, "I want us to continue this conversation further through my email which is . . ." In different emails, the exact same words are used. It looks like there's a form out there for scammers to follow. Some are not as easy to spot. Many give themselves away with too broad a list of their requirements such as looking for women from thirty-three to ninety-nine, an overwillingness to relocate, and a profession of love for you that is unparalleled by any experience in your past!

Here's one that I reported to the site management from newone2779XXXXX (again, the spelling and punctuation are as written, the email address is altered).

"Good morning lady,

"Here are you doing this great morning? Hope you are doing good my name is landon **a**nd am new here actually am new to this online dating thing and I joined this Christian dating site seeking a God fearing woman and I was browsing through and I saw your profile and I read your profile in fact I was really touched and I would love to get to know you I didn't know how to upload a picture on here please email me at landonxxxxx08@xxxxx.com just got this new email address and I would reply back with me picture nd telling you all about me takecare and stay blessed."

The email did not come from a Christian site. Obviously, the message was a form that the man simply sent from various sites. When I reported the message to the site managers, I received a thank you, and they removed the man's profile.

If you find a profile that is suspect, notify the site managers. You can do it anonymously, and you could be saving a lot of grief for the person who is not as skilled in Internet dating.

There are married people on the dating sites who pose as single. Be aware of "legally separated," which can have more than one meaning. I learned to avoid anyone so listed.

Other clues to look for include these:

1. Not available on evenings, weekends or holidays
2. Always gives a cell phone number, never a land line, even after getting to know him
3. Never extends an invitation to his home
4. The telltale band of lighter skin on the fourth finger, left hand

Lessons Learned

You're on your own out in the big world of Internet dating, and you must always put your safety first. Never make an exception even if the person appears to be especially decent. The repeated contacts and rejections are all a part of the shopping process. Recognize that first meetings can be awkward, so do what you can to make it easier for you both. Read the person's profile again just before you meet so that you can pick out good conversation items. Choose a place to meet where you will be comfortable. Have some easy stories ready to tell, but guard your personal information until you are totally convinced this is a trustworthy connection.

Be ready for disappointments. Don't rely on support from friends (this applies to soothing your broken heart or encouraging your participation in this strange pursuit). Even though your friends can be curious about Internet dating, they don't understand that the rejection is real. To them, the object of your affection is an imaginary being in cyberspace. "Real" relationships start in college, at church, in the grocery store's produce department, or at the bar downtown, right? As far as encouraging you to continue in your Make It Happen adventure: would you encourage a beloved friend to put themselves in harm's way? News stories have headlined the ugly stories of the rape and extortion cases. You're on your own unless you are fortunate enough to have a friend who is also involved in Internet dating. Maybe you could encourage a friend to join you from the beginning. Otherwise, you are on your own.

Look out for scammers and married profilers. They are out there. Remember to be alert for hints of imposters.

In the next chapter we will visit with some really fine mature people who invested in this adventure.

Chapter 9—Survey of Those Involved

Revisiting

What about all those people that Rob and I met out there in cyberspace? How did they feel about Internet dating? Were they fortunate enough to make a connection, or are they still out there looking? I couldn't help but wonder.

True to my "Make It Happen" motto, I had to find answers to those questions. I was fortunate to meet a computer guru who knew how to work miracles with these newfangled "typewriters." Derek Banas and I both had roles in a local dinner theater production. We did not appear until the end of the production, so we had a lot of time to chat and get to know each other. I found him to be interesting and admired his abilities, and he offered to help if I ever needed to set up a site.

Derek created a website and a blog on Google that offered a questionnaire about Internet dating experiences. Rob and I went back over the email addresses we had kept, knowing that contacts with these folks would be a shot in the dark. Would they remember who we were? Would we clear the junk screening?

I found sixty-seven addresses, and Rob found twenty-four from his files. We sent the following email:

"Hello again,

Leaf through the pages of your memories, and you may remember that we connected as we shopped for that just right person on dating sites. Here's hoping you are engaged in an exciting relationship that made all that shot-in-the-dark shopping worthwhile.

Internet dating is a great source for meeting the extremes of very compatible to I-don't-think-so. In order for more seniors to feel confident in approaching this new style of dating, I'm writing a how-to book that I hope will make it easier for the bashful ones to jump in and enjoy themselves. My collaborator is Rob, one of my Internet 'finds' from Cleveland.

Our web site, http://adventureswithmymouse. blogspot.com, is available over the next three weeks. It explains this in more detail and will ask you to participate in a survey that evaluates your Internet dating experience. It only takes a couple minutes unless you care to linger on the results that others have written.

We will use the statistics from this survey as verification of this dating scene by those who have lived it. Also, if you would like, please respond to this email to give me an update on what's new in your life (a private exchange, not for publication).

A warm thank you for your time and cooperation, Marti."

The People Speak

The questionnaire was simple and direct, and it allowed the participants to give a minimal answer or go into lengthy detail, whichever they preferred.

What was your goal?
Age range?
How many sites did you try?

Which site was the best?
Why was it the best?
Which was the worst site you tried?
Why was it the worst?
How long did you use an Internet dating service?
Would you recommend Internet dating to a friend?
Please rate your overall Internet dating experience.
Are dating sites fairly priced?
Did you try a free site?
If you tried a free site, which one?
What did you like best about your Internet dating experience?
What did you like least about your Internet dating experience?
Your comments on profiles.
Your comments on pictures.
Your comments on respondents.
Your advice or suggestions on screening potential dates.
Currently I am: marital status, dating, taking a break.
Any other views you would like to share?

Rob and I anxiously waited, fearing that no one would respond. Would people be hesitant about getting involved? Would our email be delegated to the junk listings? Would we even be remembered as one-time participants in their dating history? Slowly the answers came in.

Several weeks later I called Rob, excited with the number of responses. "Did you get the copy of results I emailed you?"

"Yes," he answered, "we did it! I think we have something here. Some well-done descriptions that could be of value to our readers."

"Let's go through and pull out some of the 'must have' items, such as the age range of thirty to seventy-nine. Think we have some babes looking for a sugar daddy?"

"Wait a minute. They could be seasoned cougars looking for their boy toy."

"I'll give you that! The men seemed a little hesitant to go for the marriage category. They preferred a long-term committed relationship."

"My women were quite comfortable using the word marriage. Maybe that's a result of early training and expectations."

"Could be. I was so glad to see that people were using up to five sites—made me feel normal," I said.

"Even outside the Internet dating world, we tend to go to many places to see who is available. It would not make sense to only go to the corner store to peruse the dating potentials. Too limiting."

"That's true. How about the evaluation of the dating sites? I thought that was interesting, although nothing shocking. Highly individual responses obviously depending on the success rate for each person. Did you see the wide range on eHarmony? Some felt they had the best selection of matches and others complained that the testing was too long and didn't produce good matches. One of the men commented that there were not enough active members in his area and in his age range. Another was matched with rude people and those who were not truthful in their profile. There we go again, the misrepresentation in profiles. When will they learn?"

"I was pleased to see that Senior People Meet was noted as having the best choices in the right age range. Match.com was highly rated. It gives people an opportunity to select their own choices, unlike eHarmony where it's done for you. It's that 'do your own shopping' that really has appeal. You're playing the field rather than sitting in the bleachers," Rob noted.

"And some people have been playing that field for up to five years. I wish we had asked how much time they spent on the site each day. The one-year person and the five-year person may have spent equal time on actual shopping and dating. A casual dater will probably stay on for years, but the serious 'I want to get married' person will be off as soon as that desire is fulfilled. I have interpreted 'casual dating' as never getting too involved with one person but just enjoying playing the field. Well, to each his own."

"And casual is such a safe word for us fellows to use. You know we're always sure you gals are ready to scoop us up and fly away down that long aisle."

"Dream on, my Good Knight, dream on! I'm happy that most everyone would recommend Internet dating to a friend. I counted only ten percent who found the experience to be disappointing."

"I was surprised that so few tried a free site, perhaps because they felt the other sites were fairly priced. Plenty of Fish was the leader in the free sites. No harm done in trying it. No doubt there's a lot of personal history that plays into the evaluations of sites. Success on a site—we praise it, whereas failure causes displeasure. Again, to each his own."

"Gotta run. I'll send you my reaction to the rest of the questionnaire when I have a chance to study it. I know you already did your studying. Give me a week to catch up! Sending you lots of hugs," I said.

"And to you, My Lady of the Knight, the best as always."

Survey Results

One satisfied Internet dater wrote, "It gave me a chance to meet ladies of my own age group and region, a lot more in quantity and types than any other way. It opened up a whole new relationship world for me." Another was pleased to have regained his confidence in having candid and serious discussion about his future desires with ladies who were really strangers. Perhaps this is one of the great advantages of Internet dating. So much of the "get acquainted" conversation can take place in emails and phone conversations. Many found that they could be more open in this way. No worries about appearance, bad breath, or "why didn't I lose those other ten pounds."

Of course, they also found negatives with this type dating: weird people, odd balls, callous women, the rudeness of dropping communication without explanation, fakes and hookers, dishonesty in profiles, unwilling to take the next step in a new relationship, locked into their existing lifestyle, and that terrible lie, the out-of-date photograph. Earlier I warned about the weird people. They generally give themselves away before a meeting takes place.

I have heard many comments about callous women who have become too worldly and dominating because of their independent lifestyle. They seem to be threatened by the thoughts of melting into the life of a companion. Many are women who have successfully supported themselves, reaching high on the corporate ladder . They enter the Internet dating scene only because it is the "thing to do" with no intention of a lasting relationship.

If you are into this scene for simple companionship, make it known at the beginning before someone's heart is broken. How much change can you handle? Can you relocate? Sell your house? Change jobs? Know yourself before you try to get to know someone else.

Profiles

Remember all those suggestions about writing profiles? The comments from our survey back up our advice:

- I've heard stories that indicate I was extremely fortunate to meet women who had realistic profiles.
- They list activities that they haven't even tried.
- Worthless, short profiles.
- Too many "Tell you later's"
- Dishonest about their reasons for seeking a partner.
- Insufficient information on their expectations of a new companion.

- Saying they are legally separated when they are not.
- Trying to make the information seem attractive rather than accurate.
- What does it mean, "I live each day to the fullest"?
- Too many vague comments. Be specific.
- I wish more ladies would be specific and realistic.

There you have it. There was much discontent about profiles being misleading. Perhaps we could fault the dating sites.

Should they take the lead and ask more specific questions within the profile area? Some of the sites allow blank or "tell you later" fields. (Later? There will be no later.) Women need to be more selective and demand that the profile answers be given by not responding to the men who do not give details.

How about pictures? The survey respondents said this:

- Most of the photos were misleading.
- Normally taken about five years prior.
- Pictures are a big help.
- Don't include grandchildren. I'm looking for a relationship with a woman, not her grandchildren.
- A lot of pictures were too dark and blurry.
- Right or wrong, we do tend to make snap judgments on a person's appearance.
- Varied from recent to twenty years ago.
- Some women hesitate to post a picture for security reasons.
- Some women want to appear younger by *not* posting a picture.

- Some were poorly focused.
- Some of the backgrounds divulged the messy, cluttered house where they live.
- Too few post them. They should be required.

Take the time to have a photo taken that shows you at your best. When you meet someone face to face, you will present the face you have today, not one of ten years ago. Why would you try to mask that? Remember that for every pot there's a lid. Someone, somewhere, will find you to be exactly what he is looking for.

Respondents

There was nothing earth shattering here. One respondent complained that he had a lot of no shows. Talk about impolite. If you decide not to go ahead with a meeting, contact that person. Simply tell him that you have reconsidered and you don't feel you would be compatible, or say that you have decided to go in a different direction. Don't be so rude as to not cancel.

Another respondent commented that you should "keep it light, certainly at the beginning." The warning is not to come on so strong that it indicates a do or die lifetime contract. You are simply meeting people to check them out. A second meeting may never take place, but isn't that better than a mismatch?

To give you an idea of just how extensive this search may be, one man met over two hundred women over a period of fourteen years. (Over the past year, he has settled into a relationship that he hopes will prove to be his last one. Let's hope so.) Remember this when you move into your second or third year of Internet dating. Don't settle for less than you really want.

Some sites will respond to your "must haves" by asking you to revise some of your requirements to create a larger selection of candidates. Be cautious about altering your list. You know what you want, so stick to it. Try another site. Try another day. The right one is out there.

A frequent complaint was the failure to respond to an initial overture. It takes only a few moments to write back, "No, thank you, but best of luck in your search." This allows the initiator to move on.

Advice from the Adept

Let's look at some responses about screening a potential dating partner:

- The site should only recommend people that fit the criteria set up in my profile.
- Don't drag things out in the talking stage. If the chemistry is there, meet quickly, rather than spending too much time on a nonproductive match.
- Don't go beyond half a dozen emails before suggesting a date.
- Always take the step of talking on your cell phone a number of times before setting a date.
- Remember your cell phone keeps your home identity safe.
- Be honest about everything.
- Check the other's profile again to make sure you don't have qualities listed as negative by them.

Most of these comments from the respondents were pretty standard stuff, but the "honesty" factor was the crucial one. If we could just be sure of that, there would be a lot less disappointment in Internet dating. Unfortunately, there are some who feel that they are an exception to the rule. When dishonesty is discovered, take it as a lesson, and move on.

Regarding actually meeting, there were some practical suggestions by the respondents:

- Be safe.
- Prepare for the random odd character who will slip through your prior scrutiny.
- Jump right in if it sounds right. If not, move on quickly. Don't waste either one's time.
- Meet where there are other people. Coffee shops are great.
- Meet in a shopping mall, walk casually, window shop, a great set-up for communication.
- Women must let a friend know where they are going.
- Have your cell phone with you.
- Do not meet at your home. Meet at a public place.

The first meeting will be enhanced by enjoying a museum, the zoo, or a flower show. The coffee shop is always a good bet. Just make sure that the environment allows for lots of conversation. That's what you're there for.

The majority of the respondents in our survey have found that right person. Perhaps that is why they were motivated to respond. Only one gave up, and some were still looking. Better to still be looking than to compromise.

Views to Share

Our respondents were lacking in views to share—perhaps I should credit a comprehensive, cleverly worded questionnaire that has already milked their views. There was one well-stated complaint that "the majority are too casual about their objectives and are prematurely judgmental." There you have it: the proven need to be specific in your "must haves." Make sure that you have expressed them succinctly and then stick to them in your selections and responses. Remember that not everyone can express themselves well with the written word, and some are extremely nervous carrying on a conversation with a stranger. If the "must haves" match, you will want to be careful not to judge prematurely but to give the other person a chance, whether it be with further conversations or a trial meeting.

Finale

There you have it, all the tools for a successful journey through Internet dating.

When the going gets tough, remember that the majority of people do find the companionship they seek, whether it be casual or committed. Start today to make the difference in your life. The choices are there waiting for you. All you have to do is to start the adventure with *your* mouse and Make It Happen.

Epilogue

What an interesting journey this has been for me. Thanks for coming along. I hope you learned enough about Internet dating that you will have the confidence to try it yourself.

As I relived those many days of screen watching, I was pleased with the memories of the fine men I met. Now when I sit in that rocking chair at the nursing home, I can go back and tap a memory that will put a smile of remembrance on my face and a brush of warmth across my heart. Even the not-so-fine ones were necessary on my way to a successful ending.

What was that ending? Are Rob and I living happily ever after? We are, but not under the same roof or sharing the same name. Rob is my dearest friend, a brother by mutual adoption. If two days go by without word from him, my world shutters a little until I see his words on my screen. He will always be my Good Knight, my dear, dear gentleman on call. I still send cookies to him, and we can go about six months before we need an actual visit. May it always be that way.

Who is The Right One who appeared after all that searching? It happened so easily yet so unexpectedly. Ross was widowed and still living under the shadow of his grief when he joined Match.com. My first attraction to him was the fact that he had a barber shop in Sewickley where I had spent my high school years—in fact, the shop was a couple blocks down from my old homestead. We corresponded. (Ross likes to tell inquirers that I made the first move.)

When we met, I was aware that he was feeling an uneasy guilt of being with another woman, a typical hangover from a long-term relationship. He was nice looking, intelligent, and had worked in management for Eastern Airlines after graduating from the University of Florida. He had two boys (as I did) from a first marriage and was widowed from his second marriage. We shared the exact same marital history.

You'll remember the lesson that I learned about dating men who were looking for "replacements" while still grieving, so I was not in active pursuit. I received a few more emails from Ross, and then nothing. He wiped me out of his file because I lived too far away (another part of the story he loves to tell, for now he willingly drives those twenty-five miles to work every day).

Several months later, I went to Sewickley to have a budgeting session with David, my retired financial counselor. (We didn't know it then, but David would later be our best man.) He had known Ross for many years and spoke on his behalf. As a gesture of kindness for the struggling widower, I emailed Ross to tell him that I would be in town and would stop to see him at the shop. He responded with the polite "Please do."

We had coffee and chatted between haircuts. I told him that I was going to a local berry farm to purchase my favorite wine from their new winery. Ross requested some peach wine, and I promised to get it for him. He seemed now to be much more responsive to my presence.

He came to pick up the wine and so began a whirlwind romance that would finally Make It Happen for me and define my intent. After all the sorting of prospective suitors, I found Ross to have all those "must haves" that were important to me. He is attentive, affectionate, thoughtful, generous, respectful of my space and independence, faithful to his beliefs, even tempered, family centered, and held in high regard by his friends.

Finish Line

Did I Make It Happen?
Am I really there?
Is he The One, The Mr. Right?
Are we to be a pair?

I feel content, complete.
I couldn't ask for more.
I'm satisfied to the nth degree,
All the way to my core.

Was it worth the wait,
Disappointments galore?
You better believe it,
Of that I am sure!

With Ross, there was no question but to marry. On October 25, 2009, we were married in a lovely sunflower bedecked Oakmont Methodist Church. Yes, Rob was there.

We have traveled to Ohio to see Jim (from chapter 5) and his wife. I have always enjoyed keeping in touch with Jim. He has such an amiable personality, and his writing is so quick witted. You'll remember that he was divorced from his wife and was "on the road" enjoying local scenery—that is, until his ex-wife got in touch. Ex is no longer ex! They have restored their love, which is even more precious now. It was a delight to meet her.

What about Rob, is he with someone special? Rob truly loved his wife and until the day that he finds someone as appealing as JoAnn, he will continue enjoying the smorgasbord. There are lovely women who are most happy to be on his arm for a special evening of dinner and theater.

On your way now! Go to your computer and meet your match. Be patient, be careful, and you too can Make It Happen.

In Memory Of

Martha DiGioia Kistler
March 21, 1935 - August 23, 2011

At this book was being submitted to the publisher, Marti's health suddenly declined and she passed without ever seeing it in print.

Her Internet dating "Adventures," resulted in meeting and marrying Ross H Kistler, and in finding her co-author and writing muse, Rob Ruggles.

Marti brought much joy and a fullness of life to both and to all who had the pleasure of knowing her. She is survived by her beloved husband, Ross, one son, Eric and two grandchildren, Amber and David. She is greatly missed by all.

* **

Marti DiGioia Kistler
March 21, 1935 - August 23, 2011

* **

www.ingramcontent.com/pod-product-compliance
Lightning Source LLC
Chambersburg PA
CBHW071208050326
40689CB00011B/2281

* 9 7 8 1 4 6 1 0 8 9 6 8 1 *